With sincere thanks to Potlatch Corporation, L. Pendleton Siegel III, Chairman and CEO, the University of Minnesota Duluth and its Tweed Museum of Art offer this special edition of LOOKING NORTH.

It was Potlatch Corporation—formerly The Northwest Paper Company that commissioned the illustrations reproduced for the first time in this delightful book, and it was Potlatch Corporation that donated the majority of the original paintings to the Tweed Museum of Art, University of Minnesota Duluth, in 1981. Since that time, the Potlatch Collection of Royal Canadian Mounted Police Illustrations at the Tweed Museum of Art has captured the imagination of audiences, attracting interest from all over the United States and Canada, as well.

On seeing these bold images of adventure and heroism among pristine north woods landscapes, people have inevitably asked, "Is there a book?"

At last, we are proud to say, "Yes, and here it is!"

Kathryn A. Martin, CHANCELLOR
Jack Bowman, DEAN

T W E E D
MUSEUM of ART
University of Minnesota Duluth

LOOKING

NORTH

LOOKING NORTH

Royal Canadian Mounted Police Illustrations
The Potlatch Collection

TWEED MUSEUM OF ART
UNIVERSITY OF MINNESOTA DULUTH

KARAL ANN MARLING

AFTON HISTORICAL SOCIETY PRESS

The publication of
LOOKING NORTH: Royal Canadian Mounted Police Illustrations
was made possible by generous gifts from

Lucy C. MacMillan Stitzer and Katherine MacMillan Tanner
in recognition of their father, W. Duncan MacMillan

June M. Kazeil and Mary Kazeil Anderson
in memory of their Kazeil grandparents and parents

Virginia Phelps Kendall, David P. Kendall, and Louise Kendall Dunn
in memory of Harry T. Kendall Jr., President, Northwest Paper Company (1957-1965)

Thomas and Eleanor Crosby

Anonymous

Opposite half-title page: ARNOLD FRIBERG, *oil on canvas* (31 x 30), 1953.
Frontispiece: ARNOLD FRIBERG, *oil on canvas* (32 x 37), 1943.

Edited by Michele Hodgson
Designed by Mary Susan Oleson
Printed by Pettit Network Inc., Afton, Minnesota

Library of Congress Cataloging-in-Publication Data
Marling, Karal Ann.
Looking north: Royal Canadian Mounted Police illustrations: the Potlatch Collection / Karal Ann Marling.—1st ed.
    p. cm.
Includes bibliographical references and index.
ISBN 189043454X (alk. paper)—ISBN 1-890434-56-6 (softcover)
1. Commercial art—Minnesota—History—20th century. 2. Royal Canadian Mounted Police—In art.
3. Potlatch Corporation—Art collections.
4. Art—Private collections—Minnesota—Duluth. 5. Art—Minnesota—Duluth.
6. Tweed Museum of Art. I. Title: Canadian Mounted Police illustrations. II. Potlatch Corporation.
III. Tweed Museum of Art. IV. Title.

NC998.5.M5 M37 2003
757'.3—dc21

                                      2002152832
Printed in China

The Afton Historical Society Press publishes exceptional books on regional subjects.

W. Duncan MacMillan
President

Patricia Condon Johnston
Publisher

AFTON HISTORICAL SOCIETY PRESS
P.O. Box 100, Afton, MN 55001
800-436-8443
aftonpress@aftonpress.com
www.aftonpress.com

CONTENTS

ARNOLD FRIBERG, *oil on canvas* (16 x 12), 1941. The Mountie, calmly halting his agitated horse directly in front of the viewer, is the first of Friberg's iconic Mounties—the distilled essence of strength, command, and control. The trademark dead tree punctuates the scene at the left.

PRESIDENT'S NOTE

Afton Press salutes the Tweed Museum of Art in Duluth for its foresight in preserving in its collections the Northwest Paper Division/Potlatch Corporation Collection of Royal Canadian Mounted Police illustrations, and for its assistance in publishing *Looking North: Royal Canadian Mounted Police Illustrations.*

The colorful paintings of red-jacketed heroes contained in this exciting book are enormously appealing on many levels. The illustrations are, first of all, fine examples of American commercial art, executed by some of this country's most prestigious artists, including Arnold Friberg and Hal Foster. They also tell stories of the "taming" of the Canadian wilderness and pay tribute to an institution and group of men unique to the Canadian frontier, where the Mountie has become an enduring symbol of law and order, stability, and kindness.

Hugh (left) and Duncan MacMillan, 1935.

I have long been a fan and friend of the force, dating back to my childhood when my brother Hugh and I would play "Mounted Police" in the "wild country" outside our home in Wayzata, Minnesota. We had a grand time in our small uniforms, outwitting and capturing the "bad guys."

As an adult, my connection to the force has been a real and proud one. From 1991 to 1993, I provided help to its Commercial Crime Branch. I treasure a letter I received afterward from Officer in Charge Rick Roy, which reads, in part:

Your assistance to the Royal Canadian Mounted Police . . . was a tremendous asset not only to the Force, but to the Canadian public, especially those in the agricultural industry. . . . Our investigation resulted in changes to the Canadian Grain Futures Act, the in-house Rules and Regulations of that particular business entity, and has assured the producers they are participating in a fair and equitable environment. . . .

[Your] friendship is something we value very highly. We also know we can always depend on you if and when we ever need your assistance.

So much for a childhood passion, which continues to give me great pleasure.

I hope you reap as much enjoyment from reading *Looking North: Royal Canadian Mounted Police Illustrations* as I have had in helping to bring this beautiful book to print.

W. Duncan MacMillan

PRESIDENT, AFTON HISTORICAL SOCIETY PRESS
RETIRED DIRECTOR, CARGILL, INCORPORATED

IRVIN "SHORTY" SHOPE, *oil on canvas* (32 x 25), 1960. The presence of the cougar injects a note of peril and suspense.

ARNOLD FRIBERG, MID-DAY THIRST, *oil on canvas* (32 x 25), 1964.

ACKNOWLEDGMENTS

At long last, after considerable inquiry over the years and following extensive effort and scholarship by numerous colleagues and friends, the Tweed Museum of Art at the University of Minnesota Duluth is proud to present *Looking North: Royal Canadian Mounted Police Illustrations.*

On the occasion of a premier exhibition of the same name, the Tweed Museum of Art is especially pleased to collaborate with our colleagues at Afton Historical Society Press, publisher of *Looking North,* and with author Karal Ann Marling, professor of art history at the University of Minnesota Twin Cities, to help make this impressive book a reality.

We certainly must extend our sincere thanks to the Potlatch Corporation. In 1981 Potlatch made the generous gift to the Tweed Museum of Art of 374 Royal Canadian Mounted Police illustrations, along with a contribution of $50,000 to help defray expenses for costly restoration and management of the collection. I offer my appreciation to L. Pendleton Siegel III, Potlatch chair and CEO; Franklin Carroll, former Potlatch director of public affairs; and Archie Chelseth, retired Potlatch public-affairs executive, for their dedication to and support in creating wider exposure and greater appreciation of the Mountie collection.

My sincere appreciation is extended to the Tweed Museum of Art staff, who offer exemplary professional attention to every exhibition and program detail. I especially want to thank Tweed Museum of Art curator Peter Spooner, who worked closely with Afton Historical Society Press staff and popular-culture scholar Karal Ann Marling to ensure full access to the images and to considerable research material reviewed by the author. Tweed Museum of Art technician Peter Weizenegger fabricated and installed the exhibition to the viewer's best advantage and ensured the highest-quality presentation needs and care of the Mountie collection. Kate Carmody and Cassie Wilkins, Marling's graduate art-history seminar students, designed a "north woods" installation that strengthens the exhibition's Mountie mythology and popular-culture themes. Tweed Museum of Art education coordinator Susan Hudec developed an important educational component via exhibition tours and interpretive programs. Essential exhibition support has been provided by Kathy Sandstedt, executive secretary, and Mary Rhodes, senior secretary; Kim Schandel, store manager; and security staff Nikki Bettendorf, Rose Gross, and Chong Johnson.

We are so fortunate to have such a high-caliber literary community in the state of Minnesota. Collaborating with Afton Historical Society Press, who shared our excitement early on about the feasibility of *Looking North,* made the final result even more meaningful. Our thanks to Afton publisher Patricia Condon Johnston and president W. Duncan MacMillan for their commitment to and enthusiasm for the project. Our added gratitude is extended to Chuck Johnston, Afton director of operations, for his encouragement. To Louise Kendall-Dunn, daughter of former Northwest Paper Company president Harry T. Kendall, we offer our thanks for helping to reconnect the Tweed Museum of Art to the Northwest Paper community.

I am also indebted to Kathryn A. Martin, chancellor of the University of Minnesota Duluth, for having taken special interest in *Looking North* from the onset. I deeply appreciate the support and advocacy of Jack Bowman, dean of the School of Fine Arts, and Pat Dennis, interim dean, who helped dramatically to make the book a priority and to bring it toward fruition. Ultimately, we acknowledge the sixteen talented artists and illustrators commissioned by the Northwest Paper Company/Potlatch Corporation who created the Mountie images from 1931 to 1970. These artists, each offering a unique style and interpretation, reveal the power of the image to bring to life the Mountie mythology—bold and spirited, a visual icon of universal appeal, and often revered as a highly successful agent of popular culture.

Over the years, the Tweed Museum of Art has regularly exhibited selections from the Mountie illustrations, but special interest in the images, the Mountie mythology, and the Potlatch legacy makes the long-awaited production of *Looking North* especially gratifying. For the first time, this significant scholarly study of the collection has been made available to an eager audience throughout this country and abroad. We hope and expect you will enjoy this fine exhibition and beautiful publication, *Looking North: Royal Canadian Mounted Police Illustrations.*

Martin DeWitt

DIRECTOR, TWEED MUSEUM OF ART
UNIVERSITY OF MINNESOTA DULUTH

ACKNOWLEDGMENTS

This book is based almost entirely on documentary evidence deposited at several sites in Minnesota. Peter F. Spooner, curator and registrar at the Tweed Museum of Art at the University of Minnesota Duluth, generously arranged access to the Potlatch Collection and to the research materials he has been assembling for many years. His work on the identity of the artists has been extraordinarily helpful. In Cloquet, Minnesota, Franklin O. Carroll, former director of public affairs for the Potlatch Corporation, kindly allowed my research team to explore the bowels of

14

the former Northwest Paper Company headquarters. Marlene Wisuri, director of the Carlton County History and Heritage Center in Cloquet, supplied local and industry publications unavailable elsewhere. The Minnesota Historical Society and the Minnesota History Center in St. Paul provided additional corporate documents and historical photographs of Cloquet and the forest industries of northern Minnesota. I am also grateful to Arnold Friberg for submitting to a long and probing interview and to Karl Purchase of the Royal Canadian Mounted Police for viewing the Friberg paintings for me through expert eyes.

The most important inspiration for this project has been my students at the University of Minnesota Twin Cities. A seminar offered in the spring of 2002 provided the occasion for group discussion of the Mountie pictures; in addition, several members of the seminar acted as project research assistants, while others volunteered their time and energies to help us out. Cassie Wilkins and Kate Carmody did much of the library research on Canadian history and the various uses of the paintings, and helped me to amass a formidable collection of popular films and artifacts related to the Mountie theme. David Slater, Leigh Rothke, Nogin Chung, and Kristin Anderson drove, searched, lent, discussed, and provided moral support. I am grateful to them all. Many years ago, on a summer pleasure trip "up North" with Gabe and Yvonne Weisberg, I first saw parts of the Potlatch collection on exhibit at the Tweed Museum of Art. Those startling reds have warmed my memories ever since. It has been a joy and pleasure to revisit the Mountie paintings in this study.

Karal Ann Marling

ARNOLD FRIBERG, *oil on canvas* (32 x 25), 1964.

INTRODUCTION

The Potlatch Collection of Royal Canadian Mounted Police illustrations was donated to the Tweed Museum of Art at the University of Minnesota Duluth in 1981. This series of more than 350 paintings, each featuring a Royal Canadian Mounted Police officer in his characteristic red tunic, was commissioned from sixteen illustrators between 1931 and 1970 by what was then the Northwest Paper Company, based in Cloquet, Minnesota.[1] The Mounties, as they are informally known to us, had their start as a creative and timely business-to-business advertising campaign, reflective of the northern and western forests surrounding the company's headquarters and from which the company harvested its raw materials. From nationally recognized artists like Hal Foster, Burne Hogarth, J. Allen St. John, and Arnold Friberg to illustrators about whom little is known,[2] all were connected to the Mountie ad campaign by their temporary or permanent location in Chicago, which had become a center for innovative pictorial advertising. The original function of these images was to advertise the company's papers to the printing trade. Their present function, as part of a diverse historical and contemporary collection at the Tweed Museum of Art, is the subject of *Looking North:* *Royal Canadian Mounted Police Illustrations.*

Symbolic of one particular (though vast) geographical region, and aimed at businesses rather than individuals, the Potlatch Mounties never became as widely known as some of their regional advertising-lore cousins, like the Jolly Green Giant, Betty Crocker, Paul Bunyan, or the Land O' Lakes Indian maiden. Nonetheless, these illustrations, reproduced for nearly seventy-five years on Northwest Paper/Potlatch calendars, notepads, broadsides, and print ads, have long been collected by those seeking images of the "north woods" as exemplified by the pioneering deeds of the steadfast Mountie. A stroll through any northern-Minnesota antiques shop will yield Mountie images galore, alongside rustic lodge furniture, beaver traps, birch-bark canoes, and hunting and fishing gear. Like Norman Rockwell's slices of everyday American life or N. C. Wyeth's famous illustrations for Cream of Wheat, the Mounties have now become part of the collective "popular-culture psyche." Having achieved iconic status regionally, the Potlatch Collection of Royal Canadian Mounted Police illustrations are now accessible to national and international audiences through *Looking North.*

In her entertaining and informative essay, popular-culture scholar Karal Ann Marling places the Mounties in the context of other well-known advertising images produced in America from the time of the Great Depression through post–World War II, and in the context of many popular movies, novels, and comic strips featuring Mounties. Marling traces the growth of the Northwest Paper ad campaign in great detail, from its humble beginnings as the brainchild of Chicago sales promoter Frank I. Cash to its national prominence as one of the longest-running and most successful sales promotions. For years, the company produced its familiar annual calendars featuring the Mounties and used reproductions of the paintings to promote a line of printing papers. While the Tweed Museum of Art has featured regular exhibits of the Mounties and displayed them in the context of exhibitions of its permanent collections for the past two decades, not since the time of their donation to the museum by the Potlatch Corporation have so many of the paintings, representing all sixteen artists, been brought together at one time. A companion exhibition of the original illustrations at the Tweed Museum of Art, coinciding with the release of *Looking North,* is now available for travel to other institutions.

The Potlatch Collection has alternately presented great opportunities and great challenges to the Tweed Museum of Art. The illustrations are wildly popular with viewers who prefer "traditional" narratives played out against naturalistic backdrops. The Mounties offer adventure and action at every turn, and brim with realistic detail, with nary a speck of irony or social commentary to be found. Another

segment of the contemporary public senses that those same qualities render the Mountie illustrations hopelessly and forever out of touch with the complexities of contemporary life.

Whether we're looking at Norman Rockwell's *Saturday Evening Post* covers, Hal Foster's *Prince Valiant* comic strip, the Mountie illustrations, or the anonymous work of some mid-twentieth-century book illustrator, we, as early-twenty-first-century viewers, are prone to view such blatantly innocent and hopeful images with a cynical eye. As much as we might want to, our post-WWII, Korean War, cold war, Vietnam War, Desert Storm, and now post-9/11 sensibilities make it all but impossible for us to take the heroic and bright-eyed optimism of the Mountie illustrations straight. Revisionist views of history may point out instances where art or advertising images have become "politically incorrect," and where they were used in the service of ideals or behaviors now unpopular with the current version of the society that created them.[3]

Ultimately, what is important and useful about this book, its companion exhibition, and the Mountie illustrations themselves is that they allow for reflection and discussion around these very points. Over the years, many exhibitions have taught us that America is a place both created of and shaped by compelling images.[4] These images—of landscapes and heroes and anti-heroes in the landscape—may be based on real places or events, but are soon rendered larger than life by the individual's imagination, and larger still when attached to some popular sentiment or an event that galvanizes public spirit. Whether they are advertisements or artworks in museums, we respond to such images because, even in the most jaded of us, they strike a familiar chord of desire for something solid, reliable, and worth clinging to in times of turmoil.

Some may want to view the Mountie illustrations as they would any artwork, forgetting the fact that they were first and foremost created to advertise paper products, and that in the process of doing so they fictionalized the very real character of the Royal Canadian Mounted Police officer. On the other hand, forgetting that original function means losing sight of a context that might allow us to temporarily put aside their excesses of sentiment and enjoy them simply, as Karal Ann Marling so aptly puts it, as "ripping good pictures."

Peter F. Spooner

CURATOR, TWEED MUSEUM OF ART
UNIVERSITY OF MINNESOTA DULUTH

NOTES

1. Founded as the Northwest Paper Company in Cloquet, Minnesota, in 1898, the firm became the Northwest Paper Division of the Potlatch Corporation as the result of a 1964 merger. In 2002, the Potlatch Corporation Paper Division was purchased by Sappi Paper of South Africa. Potlatch Corporation continues to develop its wood-products division, based in northern Minnesota.

2. Much new information about the Mountie illustrators was uncovered in the course of developing this book and is included with their biographies. The exact identities of two artists, however, still elude us. The signature "DeLooy" on six subjects painted between 1958 and 1960 is a mystery. It is possible the signature may be "Delong," of whom mention as an illustrator during that time period has been located. A single subject painted in 1944 by an artist whose signature reads like "Pakines" may actually prove to be that of Frank O. King. Advertising art, unlike "fine art," did not always place a high premium on originality and authorship.

In addition, seven of the sixteen artists commissioned to produce the Mountie illustrations painted fewer than ten images, and so would not become the "household names" identified with the campaign.

3. Thoroughly innocent and certainly uncontroversial when first created, the Mountie illustrations may cause certain segments of today's society to react negatively to their repeated depictions of the assimilation of First Nations peoples and to the harvesting of northern forests.

4. Most recently, the 2002 exhibition "American Sublime: Epic Landscapes of Our Nation, 1820–1880," co-organized by the Tate Britain, the Minneapolis Institute of Arts, and the Pennsylvania Academy of Fine Arts, presented a large, post-9/11 survey of the Hudson River Valley School and other uniquely American landscape painting.

ARNOLD FRIBERG, *oil on canvas* (32 x 25), 1964.

I

THE
AD
CAMPAIGN

ARNOLD FRIBERG, *oil on canvas* (32 x 25), 1970.

THE AD CAMPAIGN

One bleak Chicago Monday in January 1931, forty-year-old Frank Cash paced his Michigan Avenue office, furiously puffing on a Lucky. A trailblazer in the high-flying advertising business of the 1920s, American Tobacco's Lucky Strike brand had been the most controversial account of its day. Bolstered by testimonials from prominent athletes, tycoons, singers, and society women, copywriters claimed that the special "toasted" tobacco was soothing to the throat, that cigarettes were the dieter's best alternative to candy. The testimonials, it soon emerged, were bought and paid for. The candy trade rose up in righteous indignation. But the bull's-eye pack sold anyway, despite the garish and vulgar ads; in 1931, the president of the company took his case to *Printers' Ink,* the ad man's bible, swearing that all the movie stars featured in the current campaign had volunteered for the job for the love of Lucky Strikes.

Frank I. Cash, whose own advertising agency had been open for little more than a year, had good reason to contemplate his predecessors' spectacular triumphs and failures. The fledgling Cash and Associates— "Advertising and Sales Promotion"—was about to take on a new and challenging job for the Northwest Paper Company of Cloquet, Minnesota. Stuffing sketches and budgets into his briefcase, Cash turned

out the lights, closed the door behind him, and caught a cab to the railroad station, bound for his first face-to-face meeting with the would-be client. And in his lower berth, Cash lit another cigarette, rifled through his papers, and reviewed what he knew about Cloquet, Northwest Paper, and the problems besetting both as the Great Depression settled over the forests of northern Minnesota.

First, there was the Great Cloquet Fire. In October 1918, after a tinder-dry autumn, a devastating firestorm swept across northeastern Minnesota, destroying everything in its path: forests, homes, crops, and most of the town of eight thousand. Refugees poured east into Duluth, clinging to whatever trains could find their way through the holocaust. The National Guard was mobilized. The Red Cross set up relief stations. By the time the inferno had burned itself out, fifteen hundred square miles had been blackened, 453 people were dead, and more than twenty-five thriving villages had vanished overnight—the worst disaster in state history. According to a headline in the *Carlton County Vidette,* the city of Cloquet was "wiped out . . . with a loss of probably twenty million dollars!"

The second crisis came thirty-two years after the

founding of the Northwest Paper Company. Led by the Weyerhaeuser family, Northwest Paper was the partnership that built the first paper mill in Cloquet and produced its first run of newsprint—twenty tons a day—in April 1899. In 1930, however, Cloquet was threatened by an economic conflagration. Just as the first effects of the stock-market crash of 1929 were felt in the mills, Northwest began construction on a costly new paper machine, scheduled to come on-line in 1931. Now, with the bills coming due, there was no ready market for the high-quality bleached offset papers that Machine No. 4 was slated to produce. In desperation, Northwest's sales manager, I. L. Gartland, begged the board to move his office to Chicago, closer to the marketplace, at the heart of one of the nation's most vibrant centers for innovative pictorial advertising.

The schools attached to the Chicago Art Institute and the Chicago Academy of Fine Arts were major training centers for the cream of the industry's illustrators. In addition, the boom in advertising in the 1920s had encouraged artists to form commercial studios, from which memorable campaigns for Studebaker cars, Kohler plumbing, Quaker Oats, Camel cigarettes, and Instant Postum had emanated. Haddon Sundblom joined forces with two other artists to form Stevens, Sundblom, and Henry in 1925; this was the shop that created the famous Santas for Coca-Cola and Whitman's chocolates, and its prestigious client roster included Palmolive soap, several Procter and Gamble lines, and Maxwell House coffee. J. C. Leyendecker, future father of the square-jawed Arrow Collar Man, began his career at age sixteen in a Chicago engraving house.

Throughout the 1930s, ad agencies, publishers, and manufacturers flocked to the Windy City in search of expanded business opportunities. The J. Walter Thompson agency opened a Michigan Avenue office early in 1931, as did Young and Rubicam. And, despite the presence of active ad firms in St. Paul and Minneapolis, Minnesota concerns too felt the pull of the big city. Munsingwear knit goods relocated its sales office to Chicago as the depression cut ever deeper into profits. At the same time—January 1931—trade papers carried the news that I. L. Gartland, formerly of the Port Huron Sulphite and Paper Company and the Groverton Paper Company, had been named general sales manager for Northwest Paper of Cloquet.

Aggressively seeking fresh ideas and a competitive presence in the marketplace, Northwest and Gartland opened a new office on Wacker Drive in Chicago. Recruiting Frank Cash and Associates was their first order of business.

At 7:00 A.M., after a night of reviewing Northwest's various product lines in his Pullman berth, Cash met Gartland on the windswept station platform in Duluth. The temperature stood well below zero. The twenty-mile drive to Cloquet over icy roads took more than an hour. But at last they reached company headquarters and sat down to meet the boss, William Kennedy. Kennedy got right to the point. "Well, Mr. Cash," he is quoted as saying, "tell us how you propose to spend our $500 a month." According to legend, Cash lit a Lucky, opened his bulging briefcase, and pulled out a rough drawing of a Canadian mounted policeman breaking a trail for his sled dogs through the snowy north woods. Then he began his pitch: "We can illustrate each ad with a picture of a mountie."

Why a Mountie? To promote high-quality printing paper to the trade, the important thing was not some clever copy or witty turn of phrase. Instead, it was crucial to get a sample of the product into the hands of a potential user and to show how well it actually reproduced the intended colors—how well it "printed." Cash proposed inserting broadsides, or printed sheets bearing colorful scenes, into the major trade journals. The face of each sheet would carry a pictorial reproduction and the back side the contact address for purchase of "Pedigreed Printing Papers." The red Mountie tunic and the vivid outdoor hues of the landscape would test the printing qualities of the paper to their limits, Cash argued. The heroic male figure would appeal to the jobbers and the printers: theirs was, in the 1930s, strictly a man's world.

The first seven broadsides Cash pitched to Northwest Paper were illustrated with Mountie scenes by Hal Foster. A Canadian, a native of Nova Scotia, Harold R. Foster's (1892–1981) early claim to fame was that he had ridden a bicycle one thousand miles from Winnipeg to Chicago in 1921 to enroll at the Art Institute and the Academy of Fine Arts. By the mid-1920s, well established as an illustrator in his own right, Foster also served as an assistant to J. Allen St. John, one of the local stars of the profession. St. John, in turn, was an associate of Edgar Rice Burroughs, author of the *Tarzan* books. Through this chain of connections, Foster would drop out of advertising to take over

the syndicated *Tarzan* comic strip in September 1931. His first batch of work for the Cash agency, including the Mountie with the sled, came just before he deserted commercial illustration to launch the premier adventure strip of the century, *Prince Valiant.* Nonetheless, despite a career change, Foster continued to take on occasional work for the Northwest series until the end of World War II.

In the seminal meeting in Cloquet, Frank Cash had stressed the obvious connections between the firm and the popular image of the Canadian Mountie. There was the old name of the force, for example: the "North West Mounted Police." North West Mounties. Northwest Paper. There was the geographic connection between the Northwest Territories of nineteenth-century Canada and the American "Northwest," or what natives called the region encompassed by Minnesota and the Dakotas. Snow. Forests. Rugged landscape. And there was something intangible—the reputation of goodness, strength, and square dealing that attached itself to the men in the red coats and, Cash hoped, to the Northwest Paper Company and its products. The paper executives were convinced. And so, with a quick sketch of a Mountie in a red coat, a Canadian artist launched one of the longest-running series in the history of American advertising.

Many of the earliest Mountie images were calibrated to the sensibilities of potential buyers as hard hit by the economic slump as the papermakers themselves. The pictures showed brave men

HAL FOSTER, *watercolor* (12 x 16), 1935. The Mountie finds signs of the suspect he pursues, or, in the words of the advertisement, "Evidence that cannot be denied" of the excellence of Mountie E. F. seventy-pound book paper, on which the picture has been printed.

overcoming adversity. They shot charging bears, paddled canoes upstream against raging currents, or struggled to stamp out a trail through the deepening snow. The tag lines attached to the pictorial vignettes urged stoic resolve in the face of obstacles. "Forward—Press On!" read one such title. "Only the Strong Meet Today's Conditions," declared another. The reference to hard times—to the effects of the depression on the nation's business—was too blatant to miss.

Even before the first series of Hal Foster ads appeared, there were signs that Northwest Paper was preparing itself for a major shift in promotional strategy. In 1932, the company began mailing weekly samples of its products directly to potential customers. The samples carried "historical sketches of the Great Northwest," texts illustrated with line drawings of fur traders, pioneers, Indians, and key moments in Minnesota's past. Each page included a small-print notation specifying the brand name of the particular paper type used. In 1933, the sheets were collected in a bound booklet that forms a record of the paper lines at the forefront of the company's early efforts, namely, the Klo-Kay, Wilson, and Nor'West types. A similar booklet, copyrighted by Frank Cash in May 1932, was titled *Out of the Great Northwest.*

Records assembled by the Northwest Paper Company in the late 1930s and again in the 1960s, when other products (wild rice, candy bars, beer, and canned vegetables) began to use a Mountie logo, show that existing brand names registered in the 1920s—Klo-Kay, Carlton, and Arrowhead, for example—were gradually displaced by a new system of nomenclature when the Cash agency systematized titles, logos, and ad styles. Among the new brands registered between 1931 and 1936 were Timberland, Pedigreed, and, of course, Mountie "book papers," branded with a line drawing of a standing Mountie astride a compass and the company seal. Cash explained his strategy in a letter to Northwest's patent attorney in February 1939. "This company has expended many thousands of dollars in successfully establishing an advertising identity inseparably linked with portraying and associating itself with the symbolic character of the old-time Northwest Mounted Police," he wrote. "The name of the company itself . . . , its locale, its position in historical background, its aspirations and its conduct, were motivating factors which led us to create the 'Mountie' background for their advertising theme song."

In fact, the Mountie theme was institutionalized by fits and starts, as the corporate balance sheet permitted. The firm's annual reports for the first decade of Cash's leadership speak of "real besetting difficulties" in shifting production volume to the more expensive and profitable grades of paper identified by the Mountie, and of problems with the frequency and volume of advertising. Although Cash's budget amounted to 1 percent of Northwest's net sales in 1936, direct-mail advertising continued to be "rather sporadic," according to Cloquet executives, and "magazine advertising was spread out too thinly over too many publications to be effective." At the same time, Cash's clients realized that the process might be slow—that persistence was needed to establish new mill-brand papers and to build up a reservoir of goodwill.

The worst year of the downturn proved to be 1936. Northwest executives came and went as the paper industry struggled to right itself. But before the end of the decade, regular full-page ads in striking color were appearing month after month in the same carefully chosen journals, with "dignified and effective [copy] of a highly creditable character." And the Mountie had begun to adorn a whole range of giveaways distributed to employees, buyers, and other interested parties. These included pocket calendars, blotters, protractors, matchbooks, and, in 1939–1940, wall calendars and memo pads, using illustrations from the ads. The big calendars were Northwest's pride and joy, beautifully printed and designed, with numbers large enough to be seen across the floor of a crowded print shop. "The Mountie scenes allow of striking color effects and permit many examples of fine art and printing work," states an internal company memo. "Reprints of many of these have been in great demand for framing" as works of art.

The first calendars have been described as "rather crude affair[s]," with twelve watercolors of Mounties, each one standing for a month of the year. Yet they had captured the attention of the trade and, as the quality of the color work improved, of segments of the public at large. The housewife on her way to the market and the gentleman sorely tempted by sneak previews of next year's sedan were the usual targets of American pictorial advertising; by contrast, magazines for grocers or druggists were staid, black-and-white publications that claimed to appeal to the hard-headed businessman rather than the emotion-driven shopper. The Mountie ads cleverly confused the issue with illustrations that set sober pressmen dreaming of derring-do in the north woods and even intrigued consumers who had no stake in the paper trade. In fact, the emotional pull of the pictures harks back to a memorable and extremely effective Minnesota ad campaign of the first quarter of the century.

Cream of Wheat cereal, originally manufactured in Grand Forks, North Dakota, moved its operations to Minneapolis in 1900 and celebrated the event with a series of full-page ads in popular consumer magazines, such as the *Ladies' Home Journal* and the *Saturday Evening Post.* Prepared by the stellar advertising artists of the day—James Montgomery Flagg, Philip R. Goodwin, and N. C. Wyeth all contributed work—most of the ads involved the continuing exploits of a black chef called Rastus. But the young Wyeth deviated from that theme with three canvases full of adventure and romance,

inspired by Frederic Remington and loosely based on Wyeth's own 1904 trip to the American West.

Wyeth went out to cowboy country in the first place for purely commercial reasons; Old West and Wild West nostalgia was in full tide as modernism threatened to put an end to the last vestiges of America's legendary past. Because Remington's bucking broncos and gunslingers were being reproduced weekly in *Collier's* to universal applause, Wyeth reasoned that he should add that subject to his repertory. The best-known result of his crash course in the West was a pair of Cream of Wheat ads. One canvas showed a rodeo rider struggling to keep his seat atop a wild stallion; providentially, the name of the cereal was painted on the wall of the grandstand behind him. The other picture, *Where the Mail Goes Cream of Wheat Goes,* depicted a cowboy mailman on a lonely stretch of prairie, dropping a letter into a Cream of Wheat crate used as a postbox by some frugal settler.

But the third in the series was a "Northern"—a genre then popular in pulp novels—in which a musher defends his sled (laden with Cream of Wheat, of course) from a ravenous wolf pack. Titled *Alaska,* the encounter could just as easily have been called *The Frozen North* or *Canadian Hunter.* The endless snowfield is geographically nonspecific, but the lone figure wears the traditional sash, or *flèche,* of the French-Canadian trapper. Destroyed by fire in 1969, the 1907 *Alaska,* in its printed versions, provides a telling Minnesota precedent for Northwest Paper's later Mountie project.

In fact, Minnesota companies developed an extraordinary number of human icons or trademarks in the 1920s and 1930s, often with the assistance of Chicago ad agencies. These include the Jolly Green Giant (previously stubby and white), who acquired green skin and an impressive physique in 1928, thanks to Erwin Wasey and Company of Chicago. And the Land O' Lakes Indian maiden, also born in the 1920s. And Betty Crocker, the perfect homemaker, whose first official portrait was painted at mid-decade by *McCall's* cover illustrator Neysa McMein.

By humanizing the stony face of corporate America, icons like these aimed to make the customer relate to the product on an emotional level, whether the commodity for sale was canned peas, premium butter—or high-grade offset printing paper. In the pages of family-interest magazines, like *McClure's* and the *Saturday Evening Post,* in among other ads for Victrolas and soup, this was hardly a bold strategic move. Yet ongoing characters had the advantage of establishing an imagistic continuity, so that one ad evoked past entries in the series while their colorful treatment set them apart from duller copy and imagery used by other manufacturers. Frank Cash's bold stroke was to apply new methods of consumer advertising to the stodgy realm of business-to-business promotion.

Despite Cash's best efforts, Northwest Paper reached a desperate, sink-or-swim stage at the end of 1936. Cash and his associate, Caraline S. Pedersen, responded with a more vigorous plan of attack, involving a stable of new artists—and more

of them. Hal Foster had been chosen for the Mountie campaign in the first place because of his reputation for rendering men convincingly in an era better known for the refinement of its "pretty girl" types. But while Foster contributed occasional Mountie vignettes until the mid-1940s, it became clear in 1936 and 1937 that he intended to work primarily as a strip cartoonist. Other Chicago-based illustrators from Foster's circle picked up the slack. J. Allen St. John (1875–1960), who had been among Foster's mentors, had done many Western scenes and was also the book artist most closely associated with Edgar Rice Burroughs's he-man *Tarzan* novels; St. John was called upon for a Mountie in 1944. Another Cash/Pedersen recruit, Burne Hogarth (1911–1996), a Foster fan who took over the *Tarzan* strip in 1937, would join the Mountie team briefly in 1945. Studley Oldham Burroughs (1892–1949) was the author's nephew. He also became the illustrator of the *Tarzan* books when St. John's rates proved too high. Along with other advertising jobs, the young Burroughs did several Mounties in the mid-1930s.

Frank Godwin (1889–1959), a New York cartoonist and illustrator, completed a pair of notable canvases for Northwest Paper during World War II; one is a moody view of a Mountie on horseback, braving a snowstorm, with his parka blown back at one knee to reveal the brilliant red tunic beneath. Benton Clark (1895–1964), who trained at the Art Institute and worked briefly for the Sundblom and the Kling studios in Chicago, was a prominent painter of Western adventure scenes. His highly dramatic Mountie in the snow of 1943 is painted against a frigid blue background lit only by firelight spilling from the doorway of a cabin. Effective as many of these illustrations proved to be, however, one or two exemplary pictures could not sustain an ongoing campaign based on regular doses of a central theme, sweetened with variations on that motif, and spiced with action—but always and ever starring the steadfast Northwest Paper Company Mountie.

Two artists carried the burden after the Mountie series was revised and improved in the mid-1930s. One was Paul Proehl (1887–1965). The other—the backbone of the campaign, with hundreds of canvases and occasional layouts to his credit—is Arnold Friberg (1913–). Proehl was another alumnus of Chicago's commercial art schools. In 1924, he became a partner in Palenske Young, a local illustration studio with a prestigious address on North Michigan Avenue, where Cash's agency was also located. In the 1930s and 1940s, Proehl was perhaps best known for his railroad calendars for the Chicago and NorthWestern Railway, but he also painted dozens of Mounties during these years, some in oil, some in watercolor. His Northwest pictures share a limited palette common to works intended for magazine use before 1926, when Norman Rockwell made a splash with the first full-color cover for the *Saturday Evening Post*. Even when they are painted in color, Proehl's Mountie scenes stick to a restricted palette of grays, whites, and steel blues, with brown accents. This was an effective technique because the artist's coloristic restraint makes the brilliant red of the Mountie uniform explode from the picture with real power and force, although the narrative content is generally low-key and peaceful, all parties working together in idyllic harmony.

Arnold Friberg was another product of the Chicago advertising pipeline. Born in a suburb of that city, he grew up in Arizona and during his teenage years studied art by mail through a correspondence course from the Federal Schools of Minneapolis (later, Art Instruction Schools). In 1931, at the age of nineteen, he enrolled in person at the Chicago Academy of Fine Arts; just as Hal Foster was preparing his first Mountie sketches, young Friberg was taking classes with J. Allen St. John and learning to hero-worship Remington, Wyeth, Maxfield Parrish, and the other great illustrators of the preceding generation. After a break to earn more tuition money, Friberg returned to Chicago in 1934 and finished up at the academy. And, like his fellow graduates, he found himself drawn to South Clark Street, where art and advertising studios had rented space in among the printing plants and publishing houses of the city. Working from a free desk in one such studio, Friberg tried his hand at commercial art of all kinds, including fashion illustration and cover layouts for specialized periodicals, like *Practical Builder* and *The Brick and Clay Journal.*

One blazing summer day in 1937, Friberg later recalled, he was sitting on the floor in front of his refrigerator, its door open to provide a puff of homemade air-conditioning, when Frank Cash phoned with an invitation to Friberg to try his hand at a Mountie picture for the Northwest Paper Company. Coincidentally, the Foster ads had already captured the attention of the twenty-three-year-old novice. He was full of admiration for the memorable qualities of the relatively uncomplicated Northwest pictures, watercolors

PAUL PROEHL, *oil on canvas* (21 x 20), 1946. The ferryboat, full of passengers, makes its way across the river unimpeded.

carried out in strong reds and blacks.

On that summer afternoon, Friberg was more than ready to think about snow and cool Canadian breezes. His became the first ad in the new, improved version of the series—a spit-and-polish Mountie and a disheveled companion in a plaid shirt paddling a canoe downstream through dangerous rapids. "For better printing specify MOUNTIE PEDIGREED printing paper," read the caption. The ad ran in *Business* and *Printer* magazines, and Friberg became *the* official Northwest Mountie artist until the campaign was put to rest in 1970. Except for a thirty-eight-month stint in the infantry during World War II (when individual pictures were purchased from Benton Clark, Burne Hogarth, and others), Friberg served as the Remington of the frozen North—the man who made culture heroes of the North West Mounted Police—for the duration of one of the longest-running advertising serials in history.

His watchword was accuracy, of an oddly selective type. Canoe scenes sent him off to study a real birch-bark craft in the collection of Chicago's Rosenwald Museum, from which he made detailed studies. He rented a tunic from a local costume shop. When future pictures seemed likely to include horses, he drew from life at the National Guard Armory. In later years, research became something of an obsession—details of how the Mountie lanyard was worn, what kind of Métis beadwork was appropriate for a given article of dress, what ornamentation might grace the prow of a canoe. Instead of forming an idea of Canadian scenery from travel brochures, he trekked into the

Sierra and drew trees as they really existed. He found coaches and wagons and old tools in the historical room of the Wells-Fargo Bank in San Francisco and on the several movie ranches near Hollywood where Westerns were filmed.

That is not to say Friberg's pictures are accurate. On the contrary, he understood that his assignment was to tell a story forcibly, to arrest the eye and capture the imagination, and to assure pictorial variety within the strict confines of the commission. Narrative and the interests of a ripping good picture took precedence over specific historical events: better a stalwart Mountie tracking a miscreant through an untamed wilderness, or a Mountie mending a doll for a little girl—Shirley Temple starring in 1939's *Susannah of the Mounties*—than a correct re-creation of the 1874 Great March West or an incident in the bloody Riel Rebellion of 1885. Accuracy was cherished in minute details, as a way of lending conviction and interest to the canvas. But what counted in the finished product was romance, tenderness, action, adventure—a typical incident, a moving story—not necessarily a true story.

This was Norman Rockwell's winning formula too. Until the postwar period, Rockwell was primarily a cover artist, charged with creating eye-catching, sweetly humorous works that would sell magazines. Like Friberg's Mountie pictures, these were textless narratives describing situations in clear, often stereotypical terms: the squabbling couple, the mischievous child, the reader dreaming over a book—little stories Rockwell made up and recounted through the use of models posed to

ARNOLD FRIBERG, *oil on canvas* (32 x 25), 1964.

correspond to his idea. What made his covers for the *Saturday Evening Post* so appealing, however, was the quality and quantity of detail. Every button, every shoelace, every piece of fabric was treated with enormous respect. And the details attested to the veracity of Rockwell's observation, even when the scene was blatantly contrived.

By 1937, Rockwell had hit his stride with covers like *Gaiety Burlesque,* a portrait of a couple of down-at-the-heels hoofers slumped dejectedly on their big theatrical truck. Furthermore, virtually all of the *Post's* stable of would-be Rockwells were imitating his winning technique. Albert Hampson, Frances Tipton Hunter, Robert C. Kauffmann, Douglass Crockwell, and a host of lesser lights churned out pseudo-Rockwells, but so did his older friend and rival, J. C. (Joe) Leyendecker. Rockwell's work was a school for America's illustrators, for newcomers in particular, and it is clear that Friberg was one of his many pupils in absentia. "Looking at a Friberg painting," noted a later company press release, "it doesn't take much imagination to hear the leather creak as the Mountie reins in his horse, feel the bite of blowing snow or smell the cooking at an Indian camp." The details, combined with a colorful cast of supporting characters, give Friberg's Mountie pictures a smoky flavor of exoticism, adventure, and occasional humor comparable to the tang of understated comedy in Rockwell's depression-era *Post* paintings.

In the 1920s and 1930s, the camera was still the illustrator's secret weapon. Rockwell recalled colleagues rushing to hide all evidence of photographic intervention when fellow artists came to call. But, by the late 1930s, with professional models in

retirement and demand for work finally rising, Rockwell succumbed to temptation after a long struggle with his conscience. His procedure involved setting up scenes, complete with props, costumes, and sets built or borrowed for the purpose; these were then photographed by a professional, the prints were beamed onto canvas with an opaque projector (Rockwell used a balopticon), and the outlines traced off in charcoal. In an article written by Friberg for *The Illustrator* in 1950, he describes exactly the same process, supplemented by additional sketches and photos of bits of scenery and items of dress.

Like Rockwell, Friberg pitched his work to the agency by means of little watercolor sketches proportioned to the shape of the illustrations desired for a given campaign. "These are done without the use of models or reference material," he admitted, "in order to leave the imagination free." But whereas Rockwell was famous for arduous searches for the perfect face of a fictional postman or a schoolgirl, Friberg painted Mounties that are all very much alike—a type, or types, rather than an individual. His younger Mounties are square-chinned and straight-nosed, with faces that taper downward from a broad forehead at perfect forty-five-degree angles. The heads are planar arrangements of strong shapes, similar to those of the well-dressed gentlemen Leyendecker supplied to the manufacturers of menswear in the 1920s and 1930s. Friberg's older Mountie, the hero of works completed after World War II, is similar but wiser and a little more genial—prone to crinkling his eyes in a sign of good humor—as if the fictional character were aging and mellowing at the same rate as the artist himself.

In addition, the younger Mountie often averts his eyes from the viewer's to look down at tracks in the soft earth or to gaze across a stunning natural vista, his face effectively hidden by the pose or by the brim of his Stetson hat. The pictorial emphasis thus falls on his actions, his bright uniform, and his surroundings, or precisely the elements best suited to the needs of the Northwest Paper Company. Instead of a soap opera about the life of one particular Mountie—his varied assignments and duties—the series becomes a saga of Mountiedom, of the near-mythic status of the bold, brave men of the North in their red tunics. The story, the epic, comes straight from popular fiction and the Hollywood movies based upon it.

Many illustrators sensed the affinity between their pictorial fictions and the stories told in other media. Rockwell was frankly stagestruck: he mingled with and painted the likes of Gary Cooper and took on jobs aimed at publicizing Hollywood's latest efforts. Among the commercial artists of Chicago, Paul Proehl worked for RKO and Columbia Pictures as a sketch artist. Harold Michaelson (active 1940s–1990s) collaborated with Alfred Hitchcock and Orson Welles. Others gravitated toward the comic strips that often served as the conduit through which novels flowed into the typewriters of Hollywood scriptwriters. Arnold Friberg would later count his years in the movie colony, as a special assistant to Cecil B. DeMille, among the greatest experiences of his life. His Hollywood interlude began in December 1953. On the strength of a group of canvases depicting incidents in the Book of Mormon, Friberg was lured away from his new home in Salt Lake City to become chief artist-designer for *The Ten Commandments,* the latest DeMille spectacular.

The assignment covered a multitude of tasks. Friberg made costume sketches, later translated into fabric by famed designer Edith Head. He imagined the various roles in paint, effectively casting the picture for DeMille on the strength of the biblical figures as he saw them (Moses, played by Charleton Heston, is a Friberg Mountie in shepherd's clothing). He began a group of large oils that composed the key shots in the film for the camera. He painted the title cards and the credits shown on screen as the lights went down in the neighborhood Bijou. It was his idea to use a length of striped Hebrew homespun as the motif whereby Moses—baby, prophet, lawgiver—would be recognized throughout the film.

Friberg came away after four years on the set with a lasting admiration for DeMille, an Academy Award nomination for costume design, and a somewhat altered view of how the Mountie series ought to evolve. After 1957, the amount of physical detail in his paintings increased exponentially: Friberg dressed his work as the set decorator of a lavish production might adorn the pharaoh's palace in the interests of greater realism. How else would a moviegoer believe that his favorite detective or Western star was now an Egyptian nobleman? Friberg came to prefer the big production-number endemic to the silver screen in the 1950s, a Cinemascope, Technicolor approach to picture-making. His painted scenes became more complex, more cinematic in the DeMille manner, with greater numbers of figures and a greater variety of incidents. Virtue always triumphed, to be sure, and villains

ARNOLD FRIBERG, *oil on canvas* (33 x 26), 1964.

were always thwarted. But little by little, the stiff, stern Mountie of an earlier day became more fully human. Sometimes, when Friberg's mental script called for it, the larger-than-life hero could even break into a chilly smile.

Where did Hal Foster, Arnold Friberg, Frank Cash, and the others get their collective notion of the Mountie in the first place? Why did they assume that the U.S. public would equate the Mountie symbol with integrity, strength, and dependability? The movies were certainly one means by which the equation between the North West Mounted Police and manly rectitude was forged. Canadian writer Pierre Berton, in his well-known lament for the Americanization of somebody else's national icon, blames Hollywood: "The movie Mountie was almost invariably brave, noble, honourable, courteous, kind, and trustworthy—all the standard Boy Scout qualities, to go with the hat. . . . He is the quintessential hero and he always wins. He gets his man."

The string of 256 Mountie flicks, says Berton, began in 1909 with a one-reeler called *The Cattle Thieves* and reached a kind of romantic crescendo with the release of the 1936 version of *Rose Marie*, starring Nelson Eddy as the singing Mountie who warbles the "Indian Love Call" to Jeanette Mac-Donald at the drop of a brown Stetson hat. "Snow pictures," or "Canadians"—films set in the Arctic and the generic "Northwoods"—were particularly relished by exhibitors for the sweltering summer months, before theaters were air-conditioned. With

piles of fake snow and electric icicles in the lobby, and a load of shaved ice packed into the ventilation ducts, Mountie pictures were the perfect antidote to hot weather in the 1920s and 1930s. But the movies had their origins in best-selling fiction, comics, and radio serials.

Novels about Mounties, which were written by British, American, and Canadian authors, enjoyed a vogue from the 1880s through the 1920s. In recent years, Canadian literary historians have tried to attribute the distinctive qualities of each type to the nationality of the writer. The British-made Mountie, for example, is often said to be a displaced Englishman who carries the banner of empire like a Kipling redcoat in the Raj. Regardless of national origin, however, Mountie stories all responded to the same crisis of modernity: with the rise of corporate culture, opportunities for individual action lessened, and as they did, traditional ideas of manhood came under attack on both sides of the Atlantic. Meanwhile, city living deprived men of the opportunity to test themselves in the natural arena. A promotion to head clerk hardly compared to the feats of daring accomplished by Tarzan—or the straight-arrow Mountie of the great and mysterious Northwest, defining himself in combat with desperate characters, loneliness, deprivation, and the hazards of the trail. A kinder, gentler version of the uncouth American frontiersman or cowboy, the Mountie was inseparable from his physical environment, on the last, untamed fringes of modern civilization.

One of the most successful Mountie novelists was a Canadian from Winnipeg, Ralph Connor, a.k.a. Charles W. Gordon, a Presbyterian minister whose writings aimed to inculcate Christian values (especially temperance) into his vast readership. Connor's evangelical zeal is evident in one his earliest books, *Corporal Cameron* of 1912. The plot turns on the conversion of a young Scottish wastrel whose free spending, loose living, and penchant for the bottle exile him to Canada and a career as a manly, God-fearing, thoroughly reformed Mounted Policeman, staunch defender of the social order. Scholars insist that the quest for order and social harmony is what sets the Canadian-written Mountie novel apart from all the others. When Connor was brought to the White House to meet Teddy Roosevelt, the walking embodiment of the ideology of the strenuous life, the chief executive began to spout Owen Wister-ish clichés about the lawlessness of the Wild West. Connor was properly appalled. "Lawlessness?" he cried. "Why, Mr. President, the law runs in the western country that I know just as it does in Toronto. I never saw a man offer resistance to one of our Mounties. And what's more I never saw a Mountie pull a gun to enforce the law. . . . They are everybody's friend. They look after the sick, they rescue men from blizzards, they pack in supplies to people in need." The American—ex–Rough Rider Theodore Roosevelt, in this case—saw the Mountie as a gunslinger, a frontier marshal in a fancy suit. Connor saw the servant of an orderly society, proclaiming a rule of law before the first rancher or railroad builder ever arrived on the scene.

Connor's American counterpart was the Michigan-born writer James Oliver Curwood. In the years between 1910 and 1922, Curwood published fifteen adventure novels set in the wilderness of the Canadian Territories. Many of his books feature Philip Steele of the Royal Northwest Mounted Police (also a 1911 title), but all the heroes of his melodramas are steel-jawed titans made from the same ramrod-straight stuff as the daring Steele. Curwood had ample reason to praise the Mounties. In 1912, he was hired by the Canadian government for the princely sum of $1,800 a year, plus expenses, to "explore the prairie provinces of the West and then go up into the north to gather material for articles and stories intended to induce settlers into that country." In effect, Curwood was paid to portray the Mountie as a father figure prepared to do the utmost to protect would-be Canadian farmers and entrepreneurs. As a writer, Curwood managed to serve up great doses of sentiment counterbalanced by violent conflict, and the recipe pleased his readers. In 1920, after publishing *The Valley of the Silent Men,* a Mountie mystery, Curwood was declared the "best-paid novelist in America," despite the fact that he admitted to stealing his plots shamelessly from Victor Hugo and Jack London (whose 1900 short story, "To the Man on Trail," includes a Mountie mushing through a blizzard).

The trajectory of mass culture in the heyday of the "Northerns" ran from book to movie to comic strip, or away from literature and toward easy-to-follow pictorial representation in an age of multilingual immigration. The early novels were scantily illustrated for the most part, but true-life adventure tales based on the history of the Mounties often contained line drawings or, in the 1930s, murky black-and-white photos. Bert Caldwell and E. J. Dinsmore, for instance, both supplied lively pencil drawings for the 1931 *Murder at Belly Butte,* a book

coauthored by T. Morris Longstreth, the most pro-
lific of the force's sympathetic biographers. More
important for the formation of a clear visual image
of the Mountie was the new novel-in-pictures, better known as the comic.

One of the first comic strips about the Mounties—
Men of the Mounted—appeared in the Toronto
Evening Telegram in 1934. The most influential was
Zane Grey's Sergeant King of the Royal Mounted, a
newspaper strip published in comic-magazine form
by Dell and other firms beginning in 1937 and
subsequently "novelized" as a series of illustrated
books. The invocation of the name of Zane Grey,
the greatest of the American Western writers, no
doubt helped to boost sales, although there is little
to suggest that Grey actually wrote or even super-
vised the various yarns in which King starred. The
uncredited illustrations are masterpieces of econom-
ical storytelling, however. Each small, square picture has been reduced to its salient features: action;
a limited cast of characters; broad, telling gestures;
and a generic Mountie, tall and manly, all chest and
tunic, with a determined set to his chiseled features.
Or, in the words of the 1873 Parliamentary Act that
created the force, a man "of sound constitution, able
to ride, active and able-bodied, of good character,
and between the ages of eighteen and forty years."

Concise and concentrated, comic-book narrative
resembled the composition of a frame of film, and
the acknowledged master of that art was Arnold
Friberg's friend, Cecil B. DeMille. His sixty-sixth
movie (his first in Technicolor), *Royal Canadian
Mounted Police,* a garbled account of the history of
the force, was released in 1940. Pictorially, the film

was a lush presentation of what would pass for
Canadian atmosphere thereafter—trees, rocks,
Indians, criminals with heavy beards, canoes—
along with a showy display of uniforms, hats, and
horseflesh. Visual images like these created a stereo-
typical Canadian Mountie and implanted him in
the American psyche as one of our own.

Friberg lived for a short time in New York City
in the late 1930s and continued his work for
Northwest Paper there. He tells of searching the
clipping files of the vast New York Public Library
for pictures of real Mounties and their habitat—
and finding only the Northwest Paper pictures
that he had painted. It's a great story. But, in
fact, Mountie movie posters and comic-book art
reached a kind of melodramatic crescendo toward
the end of the depression. While sober nonfiction
memoirs, illustrated with matter-of-fact documentary photos, now took up the role of the Mounties
in extending Canadian sovereignty to the farthest
Arctic regions, a second wave of pulp fiction
entertained juvenile readers with impossible mys-
teries, doomed love triangles, and heroic deeds.
Such characters as Downey and Steele and Renfrew
and Corporal of the Mounties came back into
print with new, eye-catching covers and strong,
simplified illustrations that leaned heavily on the
comic tradition. Friberg and the other Northwest
painters of the 1930s and 1940s had at their dis-
posal all the pictorial devices a commercial artist
could want. Even if most of the writers, directors,
and artists who celebrated the deeds of the
Mounted Police had "never been north of
Chicago," as a character in one of the novels
complained, the Mountie *was* Canada in the eyes

ARNOLD FRIBERG, *oil on canvas* (32 x 25), 1960.

of observers living below the forty-ninth parallel.

Was the heroic Mountie of the North a true representation of Canada in general or of the force in particular? According to Canadian revisionists, no. Scandals involving the misuse of police power against dissident groups and the role of Mounties in subduing strikes and suppressing "Communist" activity have tarnished the public reputation of the Royal Canadian Mounted Police. By extension, recent studies have condemned the Mounties of the nineteenth century too, pointing to bureaucratic excesses and military bungling. Even the nine-hundred-mile Great March West of 1874, a cornerstone of Canada's great founding mythology, has been dismissed as an accidental by-product of bad planning and inflexible leadership. The widely published work of Henri Julien, the Montreal reporter-illustrator who made the trek with the recruits, is often viewed today as a portrait of a tragedy, not a triumph.

To understand what the Northwest campaign signified to potential buyers of Mountie Pedigreed papers and to enthusiasts who still collect Northwest Mountie calendars and memo pads today, more than thirty years after the end of the project, it seems prudent to examine the accomplishments of the Mounties from a less academic perspective. T. Morris Longstreth, summarizing the story of the first Mounties' activities in a 1953 book for young people, *The Scarlet Force: The Making of the Mounted Police* (part of a "Great Stories of Canada" series), points to the role of the force in protecting native peoples from the depredations of American traders and their "whiskey

forts," thus facilitating construction of the Canadian Pacific Railway; their protection of and assistance to pioneer settlers of the western territories; and their policing actions during the wild, gold-rush days in the Yukon. "The young man in a scarlet tunic was their friend who would not let them down," Longstreth writes of the goodwill engendered by the force. Their courtesy and helpfulness formed "a tie between the law-bringers and the people that added a warmth to their reputation to the point of affection."

In conventional parlance, the Mounties civilized the West. And they did so wearing, at first, the bellhop caps and pith helmets of Queen Victoria's red-coated empire-builders (the Stetson came later: an 1893 magazine illustration by Frederic Remington is probably the first accurate picture of a Mountie in the uniform beloved in popular culture). Among the tribes they encountered, legend held that the red coat had been dyed in the blood of the "Great Queen's enemies." Novelist Wallace Stegner described the international border in the high plains as a "color line," with the blue of American treachery below and the red of honest dealing above. Even on the blue coats' side of the line, the Mounted Police of the late nineteenth century were heroes. The *Fort Benton Record,* published in rough-and-tumble Montana, admired a force that "fetched their man every time." Over the years the phrase became the unofficial slogan of the Mounted Policeman, who "always got his man." The real motto of the force, *Maintiens le Droit* (Maintain the Right), spoke of a moral righteousness that quickly attached itself to the larger-than-life Mountie of the imagination.

"Riders of the Plains," a turgid poem printed in a Saskatchewan newspaper in 1878 and believed to have been penned by a local Mountie, explored the true responsibilities of the force in the Northwest Territories: "Our mission is to plant the right / of British freedom here— / Restrain the lawless savages / And protect the pioneer." The brave, clean-living, dutiful constable—now available as a Barbie doll, a decorative liquor bottle, the protagonist of a family board game, coasters, postcards, Friberg wallpaper, and any number of T-shirts—has come in for some satirical ribbing in recent times. *Rocky and Bullwinkle,* a TV cartoon and comic franchise of the 1960s and 1970s, made merciless fun of Dudley Do-Right of the Mounties, a classic specimen of Canadian manhood with starched underwear, an enormous chin, and a talent for foul-ups.

In episode after episode, his horse proves smarter than poor Dudley. Similarly, the hapless troop of Mounties who serve as the Greek chorus for the Monty Python "Lumberjack Song" do not grasp the implications of the singer's propensity for cross-dressing until they are crooning the final verse. But even these comic turns reinforce fundamental elements of the Mountie mystique. In 1961, when

PAUL PROEHL, *oil on canvas* (32 x 32), 1944. The Mountie makes his case to a gathering of First Nations men. The ad looks forward to postwar competition and urges the use of paper for the "advertising and sales promotion . . . material now entering the business arena. Good printing upon Good Paper is again helping prepare the way for peacetime prosperity."

Jacqueline Kennedy wished to pay a lighthearted compliment to her Canadian hosts on her debut trip to Ottawa as First Lady, she wore a tailored Pierre Cardin suit of Mountie red and wasted no opportunity to be photographed with handsome members of the force in their matching dress uniforms.

Neither Foster nor Friberg was working for a Canadian audience, of course. While a few Mounties had painted for a hobby and a few Canadian artists re-created historical actions and engagements of the force, Northwest Paper did not need historical facts. What the ad campaign needed was the sterling image of the Mountie, polished to a very high gloss indeed—or pictures that pleased, pictures that evoked pleasant associations with manly men, tangy outdoor air, and freedom tempered by a commitment to doing the right thing. Continuity, progress, strength—these were qualities that suited the social climate of the Great Depression and sustained the ad campaign through the stringencies of World War II. During the war, paper products for the commercial market were essentially rationed to meet government needs. In 1942, Northwest advertising included a pledge to obey the rules: "We seek every measure to extend our cooperation to hasten the day of complete and final Victory over the enemies of Freedom." For the duration, Northwest products were called Victory War Quality Papers. Calendars and other promotional items were printed in stark black and white. The Mountie stood at attention and saluted. The depression-bred theme of the lone rider overcoming all obstacles took on a new significance. The Mountie was not a GI in military fatigues but he conjured up visions of one—a son, a husband, a father—doing battle in Normandy, Anzio, or the Pacific. The Mountie of the early 1940s was a scout, a lookout, a tracker, a sentry, a vigilant protector keeping watch in his lonely camp.

But the vast majority of the Mountie paintings came in the expansive period of economic growth after World War II. The paper business boomed, along with sales of new cars, new houses, and consumer durables. Far from being the exception, high-quality color graphics came to dominate the world of advertising. All of these factors left their mark on the overall style and iconography of the Northwest Paper series. A certain visual and emotional austerity notable in the wartime vignettes by Paul Proehl and other artists of the Chicago school gave way to lively, multifigural scenes in which the Mountie was integrated into a society that suddenly included traders, trappers, miners, farmers, sailors, blacksmiths, Native Americans, children, small animals, and women. In an era of domesticity and "togetherness," Harold Michaelson and Walter Oschman (active 1943–1960) specialized in variations on the theme of families visited by happy, smiling Mounties. Even Friberg began to explore other aspects of the Mountie's duties: his principal actors now guided wagon trains, protected the Canadian Pacific right-of-way, performed marriages, tended to the sick, and occasionally took part in frontier musicales.

Some of these changes began to emerge even during the years of wartime restraint. But the late 1940s and the 1950s welcomed a far greater range of expression within the outlines of the Mountie theme. Indian customs and artifacts came in for close-up study, as did the engines, riverboats, and farm implements of the western provinces. Action became more exciting. The red-coated hero grimly pursued desperadoes through more than one painting, in a kind of cinematic take on the serial narrative. He ventured more frequently into the icy stretches of the far North, where fresh dangers lurked. These fables in paint bore a noteworthy resemblance to the format of *Sergeant Preston of the Yukon,* a popular radio serial of the 1940s that moved to the CBS television network in 1955. The voice-over at the beginning of the show remained the same in both venues: "Sergeant Preston of the North West Mounted Police with Yukon King, swiftest and strongest lead dog breaking the trail, are in relentless pursuit of lawbreakers in the wild days of the Yukon. . . . On, King! On, you huskies!" Regardless of artist, the Northwest ads began to take on the suspenseful aura of the Saturday-afternoon serial, in which every episode finished with a cliff-hanger and left the audience gasping for more. Comic relief and a little genteel romance rounded out every segment. The twelve-chapter Republic Pictures *Canadian Mounties vs. Atomic Invaders* (1953) made the Mountie into a cross between Davy Crockett and Dick Tracy, with lots of fake snow and bad guys for atmosphere.

Of the sixteen illustrators who worked on the Mountie campaign, only Arnold Friberg seems to have used his regular commissions as a platform for personal development. His Mounties were splendid physical specimens—six-footers, well-muscled, with a minimum chest measurement of thirty-five inches. He paid close attention to the intricacies of headgear, boots, tunics, and tack. Verisimilitude became the hallmark of his mature style. And his landscapes are alive with local color, albeit not always that of the prairie on which the force first secured its reputation. Friberg preferred the mountains of the American West—Arizona, Colorado, California—and particularly the tree-covered peaks within sketching distance of the Utah studio he had established in 1950.

One signature characteristic of a Friberg forest is a dead tree. Often the only diagonal point of emphasis, the tree "helped in the illusion of motion" in his compositions, he believed. But it was a favorite emblem of the romantic painters of the early nineteenth century too: Thomas Cole and the American landscapists of the Hudson River School made the blasted tree—dead or dying, stripped of foliage, gnarled and misshapen—an emblem of endurance and strength, of the significance of nature's force in the life of humankind. The trees of Friberg's un-Canadian "Mountieland" of the imagination function in much the same way, universalizing a symbol and detaching it from strict Canadian and historical contexts.

During the 1950s, however, events conspired to bring Friberg back to an acute consciousness of twentieth-century America, its go-for-broke business ethos, and its unique demands on the commercial artist. In addition to his other work—a contract for Western scenes for the Louis F. Dow Calendar Company began in 1948—the pace picked up at Northwest Paper: Friberg found himself turning out a major picture every month or so. The firm, in the meantime, came to understand that the Mountie campaign was crucial to its ongoing success. In the mid-1950s, an informal audit of the swollen advertising budget showed almost $25,000 yearly being spent on memo pads alone. Magazine inserts now went into a half-dozen pricey journals every month. Between the artwork and the printing, the expenses for an annual calendar neared $50,000.

By the time the Mountie series ended in 1970, Friberg estimated that he had made $300,000 from selling his work to Northwest. But the tempo was killing: a week for a small piece and a month for a large oil, in addition to other commissions. "In 1934 *[sic]* the Northwest Mountie was made part of the Company's national advertising program," read an announcement in a trade-show program. "It has been used with increasing impact ever since. The application of the subject is virtually limitless—whether in pictures or in words. When you see the Mountie, you will be reminded that—*Northwest pedigreed papers always make good printing better.*"

Northwest Paper filed to renew the Mountie trademark in July 1953, and then set about making a complete inventory of Mountie paintings and other promotional art scattered among its offices in Cloquet, Chicago, St. Louis, and elsewhere, or on loan to important customers. At the same time,

PAUL PROEHL, *watercolor* (15½ x 15½), 1943. The Mountie takes a break from his surveillance of the woods to share a spartan meal with a squirrel—and Northwest Paper reminds readers that its products are "serving on many 'fronts' in contribution to America's war effort."

made of the dollar value of each work. These records provide fascinating insight into the worth attached by the company to different artists, media, and kinds of material. Watercolors and graphics in general were much less highly prized than oil paintings. Old works—the earliest Fosters, for example—were assigned much lower price tags than recent ones. And among the artists, Friberg commanded the highest fees, followed by Harold Michaelson, Walter Oschman, and Paul Proehl. Many extraneous factors influenced these judgments. The paper executives were more impressed with large, brilliant oils than with more modest works in fewer colors. The simplicities of the first Mountie images surely seemed crude when compared with the broader range of iconography and the sheer surfeit of detail in recent pictures. Artwork from the 1930s and 1940s had come in for hard use in printing plants and office settings, and showed its age. But the preference for Friberg's version of the Mountie is strikingly apparent.

In the meantime, Friberg became more and more interested in the Royal Canadian Mounted Police. For most of the 1950s, his knowledge of the force came from popular sources; a photograph of the artist taken in 1953 shows him posing in Mountie cold-weather gear like a would-be Sergeant Preston. But a decade later, Friberg made the first of many research trips to Canada. In Winnipeg, Manitoba, he got his first look at a live Mountie. In Regina, Saskatchewan, he learned that members of the force were avid collectors of his Northwest calendars, and he made contact with a local photographer who specialized in portraits of Mounties astride their

favorite horses. Using these photographs as guides, Friberg achieved a new depth of realism, especially in depicting uniforms. In January 1973, for an observance of the centennial of the force held in Yellowknife, in the Northwest Territories, he lent a number of his best Mountie canvases. In return, Friberg was named the only American honorary Mountie and presented with an authentic Mountie shabrach, or military saddle blanket. The horse and the blanket, shown so that every sinew and stitch could be identified, were already staples of his pictorial formula for a proper Mountie.

When questioned about his pictures, Friberg always deferred to the judgment of his growing circle of Canadian friends and was pleased when they discovered no blatant "errors." The central mistake—the red dress uniform worn on all occasions by the constable in the ads—was a forgivable function of the corporate commission. Since the Mountie brand name was the point of the ads, the man himself had to be recognizable by the things the tourist knew best. Summer and winter, in fair weather and foul, his scarlet coat had to be on show—an out-of-date uniform, circa 1925, when the Mountie's kit had reached what to the eyes of the painter was a state of aesthetic perfection. The Mountie, of course, existed in a state of absolute physical perfection, while the variety of circumstances in which he found himself hinted at a comparable spiritual excellence. In the 1960s and 1970s, as American culture reeled from one glaring excess, from one social and political catastrophe to another, Friberg's hero remained untouched and pure, a paragon and, ultimately, a soothing fiction in the era of Vietnam. The Mountie was as quaint and as distant to this epoch of hippies, assassinations, and civil rights as an armored knight in a storybook. And paradoxically, that might be why the Mountie managed to survive, despite the formal end of the Northwest Paper campaign.

In 1964, Northwest Paper became a division of the Potlatch Corporation. Under new management, the Mountie pictures kept coming at first. But in 1970, it was decided that the paintings already in hand would satisfy the needs of the company for years to come. Arnold Friberg, who was the only Northwest artist still under contract at this point, had already reached an agreement that allowed him to retain some Mountie canvases while assigning the rights to reproduce them to Potlatch. Pictures still in his studio were now completed over a period of several years: in 1973, his last Mountie was shipped off to press and the artist moved on to the genre of Western art, which had been steadily gaining in popularity. Dance halls and bad men flourished in the pictorial places where log cabins and stalwart men in scarlet had once held sway.

Mountie calendars and memo pads continued to be issued to a growing circle of fans: retired Mounties, residents of the towns where Northwest Paper had a strong economic presence, print shops—and a new class of collectors who prized popular and commercial art for its own sake. The huge Potlatch Collection promised to supply colorful Mounties for decades to come. But the custodians of the pictures also realized that their corporate offices were ill-suited to the conservation and exhibition of works of art. Many of the paintings of the 1940s and

1950s had been executed on flimsy stock; over the years, rough handling as well as extremes of heat and cold had taken their toll. Public requests to see Friberg's work were on the rise. In October 1980, the Potlatch Corporation donated its cache of original Mountie paintings—349 in all—to the Tweed Museum of Art at the University of Minnesota Duluth. "We want to share the collection, and its enjoyment, with the people of Minnesota," CEO Richard B. Madden said then of the paintings, which dated from 1931 to 1970 and spanned sixteen artists, with almost two hundred Fribergs alone. "People in the company gave the Mountie image a lot of credit for helping them weather the depression. We still use the name, and the Mountie, and you can understand why we are so pleased that these historic pictures will have a good home."

In acknowledging the de facto existence of a Potlatch Collection, Madden was following the lead of other companies that used art as a sophisticated form of public relations. Nabisco had absorbed the Cream of Wheat Company in 1961, and the parent firm in turn donated the well-known Cream of Wheat pictures by N. C. Wyeth and Philip R. Goodwin to the Minneapolis Institute of Arts in 1970. Corporate America was quicker than the museum establishment to see both the aesthetic and nostalgic value of advertising imagery from the so-called golden age of illustration, when distinctions between the fine arts and the commercial work that circulated freely in popular domain were far less rigid than they seemed to be a half-century later.

In the 1930s, when the Northwest Mountie series began, several important American businesses began to form landmark collections subsequently exhibited or reproduced in ads to enhance the prestige of the corporation. IBM and Abbott Laboratories bought and commissioned works of art pertinent to their interests at this time. For the second season of the New York World's Fair, in 1940, IBM purchased and showed works by artists from each of the forty-eight states—paintings thought to "reveal the character of these States," just as the Mountie revealed the character of Northwest printing papers. The IBM collection was part of the regionalist movement in American art, an ideological revolt against New York's dominance of art-making, artistic subjects, and critical judgments. The midwestern themes adopted by Grant Wood and Thomas Hart Benton are usually held up as prime examples of regionalism. But in their own way, the Northwest Mounties also represent a kind of Chicago-bred non-Eastern regionalism grounded in old-fashioned values, in nature, and in a readable style of painting.

These were not pictures for connoisseurs. They were intended to turn the heads of printers and publishers and businessmen with no stake in the rarefied world of the Madison Avenue gallery. These were pictures for the same people who guffawed over Wood's dour farmer with the pitchfork. The farmer was a fine example of what was called American scene painting, or pictures of familiar, recognizable, even stereo-typical slices of local color. The Mountie was just another category of regionalism—not the idyllic Iowa scene or the rollicking Missouri scene, but the imaginary Canadian scene of pulp fiction, comic books, Hollywood, and the radio serial.

Other companies hired famous artists to add a touch of class to their ads: Georgia O'Keeffe went to Hawaii on behalf of Dole pineapples; Rockwell Kent's designs sold pianos, diamonds, and dinnerware; Ben Shahn worked for the Container Corporation of America. The Potlatch Collection, although it is not made up of works by the "name" artists of our time, is an important one precisely because the campaign was not aimed at prestige, but at achieving a broader appeal, grounded in the popular culture. The Mountie wore his heart (and ours) on his bright red sleeve: he stood for integrity, bravery, and a whole range of Victorian virtues that had been banished from the abstract art of the modern twentieth century.

The Mountie was didactic but also romantic, a figure who rode off into the crisp air of the forest or the dangers of a frigid night and invited us to come along, to remember the voice of freedom that echoed from the mountains, that babbled in the fishing streams, that whispered its name in the gentle snowfall, if only in the movies or in the imagination. The Mountie brought with him the intense pleasure of recognition. He reminded us of the plangent loveliness of a spot of red poised against the tranquil greens of pine trees. In the Mountie series, today's viewer recaptures some of the oldest joys afforded by the work of art: harmony, familiarity, emotion, suggestion, empathy, memory—and a longing to be there, in the sacred grove where the spirit of the Mountie forever rides, unafraid. Where something more than justice triumphs. Where the Mountie is just as good as his slogan: *Maintiens le Droit.*

ARNOLD FRIBERG, *oil on panel* (32 x 27), 1960.

ROBERT ADDISON, *oil on canvas* (32 x 25), 1960.

II

THE
PAINTINGS

All measurements are given in inches; height precedes width. Formal titles are given when specifically listed in Northwest Paper Company or Potlatch Corporation records. Otherwise, works have been inventoried in these sources only by general descriptions of subject matter: that is, "Mountie and guide in canoe," etcetera. Unless otherwise indicated, pictures have been dated on the basis of copyright information printed in the ads using the images or through various lists of artworks maintained by their corporate owners. In cases where works are unsigned, attributions have been made using notations in inventories or in the ads themselves.

HAL FOSTER

The Beginning of the Mountie Campaign for Northwest Paper

HAL FOSTER, *watercolor* (10 x 15½), 1931. This image first appeared at the top of a text-heavy business-to-business magazine ad for Pedigreed Printing Papers, emphasizing the importance of good printing paper to modern advertising.

HAL FOSTER, *watercolor* (14½ x 22½), 1932. Featured in an ad for Northland Book Papers, the picture is described in the copy: "History chronicles the unswerving devotion to duty of the traditional guardians of the Great Northwest. Dependable service under any and all conditions was their creed."

HAL FOSTER, *watercolor* (12½ x 16½), 1932. The vigilant Mountie is linked to the message of the ad by a headline that reads, "LOOKING FORWARD. . . . The past is an open book to all, but the mist of uncertainty will always veil the future. This is just as true of the paper industry as of any other human activity."

HAL FOSTER, *oil on canvas* (24 x 36), 1932. This is the only painting in the collection without a Mountie. In the finished ad, placed in *Business* and *Printer* magazines, the picture appeared as a framed painting—above the title "THE PIONEER SPIRIT STILL LIVES"—in North Star Offset lithographic paper. At this stage in the evolution of Frank Cash's ad series, the emphasis is still on the Great Northwest and its history rather than on the lore and legend of the North West Mounted Police.

HAL FOSTER,
watercolor with pasted photograph
(13 x 16), 1931.
The grim expression of the Mountie
facing a swollen stream typifies the
depression-era theme of the lone
individual determined to succeed
against all odds.

HAL FOSTER, *watercolor* (16 x 14), 1937. In 1937, it became clear that Foster had other interests to pursue. At this point, Arnold Friberg, E. J. Boecher of Chicago's Bielefeld Studios, and Paul Proehl all became involved in the Mountie series.

HAL FOSTER, *oil on paper* (24 x 36), 1933. "Only the Strong meet today's conditions," states the caption under this Darwinian scene of struggle and danger. "In trying times of transition, the strong prove their strength, the weak make way for hardier spirits."

HAL FOSTER, SEASON'S GREETINGS, *watercolor* (16½ x 25¾), 1939. This is among the first of the Arctic scenes in the series. Much factual material published about the Mounted Police in the 1930s stressed their role in exploring the North and enforcing Canadian sovereignty among the First Nations peoples.

HAL FOSTER, *watercolor* (21 x 12), undated. By today's standards, this picture would be unacceptable on the grounds of sexism and imperialist overtones. In the 1930s, for a predominantly male audience, it was probably a kinder, gentler version of a pinup.

HAL FOSTER, *watercolor* (14½ x 12¼), 1936. This vignette is the first of Foster's surviving works to have been used without explanatory text. The protective Mountie figure now speaks for himself—and for Northwest Paper Company of Cloquet, Minnesota.

THE PREWAR PERIOD

Years of Transition

E. J. BOECHER, *ink and wash* (15½ x 17½), 1937. The Native American is removing a pack of furs from the canoe; the text underneath discusses "international commerce" and Northwest Paper's indirect role in "diversified industries."

E. J. BOECHER, *ink and wash*
(14¾ x 15¾), 1937. A rare ad for
Mountie English Finish book
paper refers obliquely to the understated vignette of a Mountie tend-
ing to his sled dogs by noting the
suitability of the stock for printing
halftones and flat tints.

PAUL PROEHL,
line drawing with watercolor
(19 x 18¼), 1939. This scene later
appeared in a wartime ad: "While
Victory is ahead, it is the considered
judgment of our military leaders that we
have before us a long, hard and costly
fight." This is the first Northwest picture to suggest that the Hollywood
Mountie was its model—or the popular
Western with a Mounted Policeman
grafted into the foreground.

PAUL PROEHL, *watercolor* (15 x 13), 1940. The Mountie's native guide (or adversary) added local color to movies about the exploits of the force.

PAUL PROEHL, *watercolor* (21½ x 18), 1940. The first of Northwest Paper's Mounties in a clearly contemporary setting, he pulls back his fur coat so that the red tunic is clearly visible.

ARNOLD FRIBERG, *opaque watercolor* (20 x 18), 1938. This painting, created toward the end of the depression as business conditions took a turn for the worse, was shelved until 1942, when the subject matter suggested a soldier scouting the terrain ahead. Northwest's wartime advertising was chiefly intended to keep the name and image of the product in the mind of potential buyers. Ad copy spoke of self-denial and the diversion of supplies to military uses. Only "essential" commercial needs could be met by manufacturers.

ARNOLD FRIBERG, *opaque watercolor* (29 x 22¾), 1940. This work too was held until after Pearl Harbor, when the lighthearted content did not match the copy, which spoke of a sudden lack of salesmen (caused by military enlistments) and the consequent need for more print advertising. The signature at the lower right reads "A. Freberg." This suggests that the picture may have been signed in absentia by someone who had heard the artist's name spoken (say, "Fray-berg") but had not seen it written correctly.

ARNOLD FRIBERG, *watercolor* (16½ x 16¼), 1940. Under this gentle genre scene, huge letters spelled out the name of "MOUNTIE" printing papers. A subject like this one would prove unacceptable during World War II.

ARNOLD FRIBERG, *watercolor* (15 x 11½), 1940. The emphasis on the setting and on historical details, like the proper construction of the Conestoga wagons in the background, is an important feature of Friberg's mature style.

ARNOLD FRIBERG, *watercolor* (22 x 18), 1941. The contrast with the small, timid child makes the Mountie look even more imposing.

MINNESOTA'S MOUNTIES GO TO WAR

PAUL PROEHL, *watercolor* (14½ x 14), undated. An early wartime picture enlists the Mountie in the cause, as he explains a map to an aviator. "Printing and its sidekick Paper have certainly 'won their wings' in the Nation's war effort . . . ," insists the text. The "sidekick" term comes straight from movie serials, and, despite his red uniform, this Mountie is an American hero.

PAUL PROEHL, *watercolor* (18¾ x 18¼), undated. The seated Mountie, pipe in hand, does not seem especially warlike, but the ad discusses the role of paper products in "informing and teaching the folks on the home front." The old settler who has put down his ax to talk to the Mountie is one of the "folks."

STUDLEY BURROUGHS, *watercolor* (15 x 15¼), 1942. A hint of romance as the pretty Indian maiden mends the Mountie's glove suggests that Burroughs saw *Rose Marie.* This is also an example of the discreet cheesecake of the 1940s.

FRANK GODWIN, *watercolor* (25 x 15¾), 1942. The lone Mountie in the snow (with his dress uniform exposed to view) is a stoic, stouthearted warrior, intent upon his task. The extreme conditions under which GIs fought overseas began to be reported to the home front in 1942 and 1943.

ARNOLD FRIBERG, *watercolor* (19½ x 17¼), 1942. A lively subject later reworked by the artist, the Mountie waving at the logging train was paired with a paragraph about keeping "the home fires burning." Recently, the artist admitted how difficult it was to find situations in which the Mountie could do more than wave at a passing train and still preserve his rather stiff dignity.

ARNOLD FRIBERG, *watercolor* (19¼ x 17¼), 1942. The pioneer woman is startled as the Mountie appears in the dark of night. The picture manages to suggest the dangers faced by the American family and the benevolent armed forces who watch over them.

ARNOLD FRIBERG, *watercolor* (19¼ x 17¼), 1942. The Mountie visits a busy trading post to offer a sober admonition to the owner. The ad warns that "in the national emergency, 'brightness' will be somewhat reduced in the interest of chlorine conservation."

ARNOLD FRIBERG, *opaque watercolor on board* (19½ x 17½), circa 1942. This dramatic night scene of the Mountie making his solitary camp in the wilderness accompanies an admission that "we'll all need a lot of fortitude . . . to win."

ARNOLD FRIBERG,
oil on board (19¼ x 17¼), 1942.
A scowling Mountie takes notes on
what looks like a Northwest Paper
Company Mountie memo pad.
Giveaways from advertisers will be
"put to good use," the text insists.
"Use more printing as a patriotic
part of your own war program."

PAUL PROEHL,
watercolor (14 x 14), 1943.
The trademark Mountie, with his
uniform on display, watches a
happy Inuit cleaning fish above
the copywriter's discussion of
"limited production, freezing
models, . . . rationing and various
other wartime restrictions."

BENTON CLARK, *oil on canvas* (30 x 33), 1943. The introduction of oil painting as the backbone of the series permitted a greater range of coloristic effects. Here, the icy blue of the snow pack creates a sharp contrast with the warmth of the light spilling from the cabin and the Mountie's blazing red uniform. In an example of self-sacrifice to duty, the Mountie and his scout leave the fireside and head off into the frozen wilds.

FRANK GODWIN, *watercolor* (23¼ x 17¼), 1944. In this modern scene, a plane airlifts supplies to Mounties snowed in in the far North. Air drops and parachutes were commonplaces of war footage shown in newsreels of the period.

PAKINES (?),
POSSIBLY FRANK O. KING,
watercolor (18½ x 15¾), 1944.
The picture shows a very spiffy
Mountie feeding a bear cub from his
skimpy ration of chocolate.

PAUL PROEHL,
watercolor (20 x 20), 1943.
Is the Mountie on the lookout for
enemy aliens? "More advertising
support of important war campaigns is needed," the ad remarks.

J. ALLEN ST. JOHN, *watercolor* (23 x 17½), 1944. A work by one of the leading figures of the Chicago illustration community, this is a conventional Wild West scene with a Mountie added for commercial expedience. The buffalo hunt inspired the copywriter to wax poetic about "the hunt for practical perfection in printing papers [that] leads . . . to the mill-brand products produced at Northwest."

HAROLD MICHAELSON,
watercolor (14 x 14), 1944.
The Mountie watches as modern-
day loggers load their truck; the
ad speaks of a "vast job ahead"
and manufactured products for
"civilian use" once the war is over.

STUDLEY BURROUGHS,
watercolor (16 x 12), 1944.
This image of the Mountie in the Arctic territories is
mythical in that he wears the cold-weather fur hat and
gloves but has discarded his parka in favor of the dress
uniform, treated in some detail.

PAUL PROEHL, *oil on canvas* (22 x 24), 1944. A calendar picture for 1945, the brilliant color and the burst of northern lights in the background presage the end of the war—and the dawning of a new day.

PAUL PROEHL,
watercolor (19 x 18½), 1944.
The Mountie relaxes and surveys his world.
The message is that "in the wake of today's
world conflict, total Victory for the United
Nations will again open peacetime channels
for paper distribution." It is possible to trace
the progress of the war in Europe and the
Pacific simply by reading the Northwest
Paper Company advertisements.

PAUL PROEHL,
ink wash (16½ x 15¾), 1944.
The Mountie fishes the logger out of
the water before the logjam comes
crashing down. The analogy is to a world
"plunge[d] abruptly to a sadly chaotic
status" but now on the mend with the
help of "Northwest's skilled craftsmen."

PAUL PROEHL, *watercolor* (23 x 17), 1944. One of the first of the popular tracking scenes reaffirms the adage that the Mountie always gets his man. The ad compares the work of the peace officer to that of the papermaker hamstrung by shortages and regulations: "The old-time Northwest 'Mountie' carried on against all handicaps and made good if humanly possible."

BURNE HOGARTH, *watercolor* (16 x 12), 1945. Peace comes to the Great Northwest.

PAUL PROEHL,
watercolor (20 x 20), 1945.
Peace again! Like the Mounties,
Northwest papers have earned
"a traditional status—that of
superiority in their class."

PAUL PROEHL,
watercolor (13¾ x 14), 1945. Mountie
and surveyor, working together to
rebuild civilization. "However, but few
significant advances have been made
that did not owe much to Paper; some
entirely due to it."

HAROLD MICHAELSON, *oil on canvas* (29 x 28), undated. The Mountie and his north-woods allies have worked together in troubled times.

PAUL PROEHL, *watercolor* (19 x 18½), 1945. Salvage efforts on the home front have won the war. The Mountie waves the stagecoach through the pass and into a bright, new future.

ARNOLD FRIBERG, *oil on canvas* (30 x 30), 1953. There is much unavoidable repetition in a series that hinges on the viewer's ready recognition of the meaning of the picture. Painters who worked in Hollywood (or those later chosen for such work) were well adapted to the chore of finding picturesque scenes that the movies and other mass media had already made familiar to the public. Surveyors, for example, were a staple of how-the-West-was-won films: they often stood for progress and modernity.

PEACE
AND
PROSPERITY

ARNOLD FRIBERG, *opaque watercolor* (20¾ x 27¾), 1946. In terms of the actual history of the Mounted Police, the subject of greatest interest becomes the role of the force in the peaceful settlement of the Canadian West.

ARNOLD FRIBERG,
oil on canvas (25 x 27), 1946.
Turning to the pursuits of peace,
the Mountie delivers the mail to a
settler and his son. Cabins, women
and children, town life—all became
part of the Mountie's biography in
the 1940s and 1950s. The scenes
echo the preoccupations of painters,
like Friberg, recently returned from
service in the armed forces.

ARNOLD FRIBERG,
watercolor (18 x 24½), 1947.
In many of Friberg's works,
there seem to be faint
allusions to real historical
events, such as Sitting Bull's
flight into Canada in 1877
with his band of Sioux exiles.
A modern-day Mountie looks
back into history from the
opposite shore of the lake.

ARNOLD FRIBERG, *opaque watercolor* (19 x 24¾), 1947. This and Friberg's other scenes show Native Americans' dealings with the Mounties as rational and pacific, unlike the violence prevalent in John Ford's postwar Westerns about American pony soldiers on the frontier.

ARNOLD FRIBERG, *opaque watercolor* (18 x 27), 1947. The uniformed Mountie and his Indian scout in buckskin and richly decorated moccasins are equals as they play with their horses on the outskirts of a settlement.

HAROLD MICHAELSON, *oil on canvas* (38 x 32), 1947. A calendar picture for 1947, this dramatic scene recalls recent organizational meetings for the formation of the United Nations, uniting former enemies in a new harmony.

HAROLD MICHAELSON, *watercolor* (22¼ x 20), 1948. The postwar Mountie often smiles in a friendly way at the trappers and loggers he visits.

ARNOLD FRIBERG, *oil on canvas* (24 x 30), 1948. As opposed to the somewhat grim camping scenes of the war years, the curious animals (see Walt Disney's *Snow White* of 1937) and the Mountie's benign expression make for a cozy, happy atmosphere.

HAROLD MICHAELSON, *oil on canvas* (25¼ x 26¼), 1948. The happy Mountie greets two boys swimming in a creek. A pleasant genre scene adapted to the needs of the Northwest campaign by the ubiquitous uniform, this leisure-time subject matter is also typical of Norman Rockwell's postwar period.

HAROLD MICHAELSON, *oil on canvas* (31 x 30), 1952. A surprising number of Northwest Paper images created during the 1950s—the heyday of the "adult Western"—make the Mountie into a north-of-the-border version of a cowboy.

HAROLD MICHAELSON,
watercolor (24¾ x 26¼), 1948.
In the late 1940s, Northwest dispensed
with explanatory comments in the
Mountie ads. Pictures like this one were
called upon to explain themselves, unaid-
ed by text. The result was simple imagery,
often with a dose of mild humor. The
infants and children of the baby-boom
generation are frequent subjects.

HAROLD MICHAELSON,
tempera on panel (27 x 21), 1948.
The new interests in pets and children
and the appurtenances of domesticity
went hand in hand with the cowboy-and-
Indian craze in children's toys.

HAROLD MICHAELSON,
oil on canvas (29 x 28), 1950.
The settler's busy wife is an important presence in this picture, just as she was on the "crabgrass frontier" of American suburbia in the 1950s.

HAROLD MICHAELSON,
oil on canvas (31 x 30), 1952.
As befits commercial mascots, the Northwest Paper Mounties are deeply involved in trade, especially the fur trade carried on in the territories inherited by Canada from the Hudson's Bay Company. The North West Mounted Police was founded to deal with American wolf-skinners whose poisoned bait also killed the animals hunted by the Blackfeet and other tribes. At Fort Whoop-Up, unscrupulous American traders bought Indian furs for the price of a cup of bootleg liquor, creating tensions on the plains.

ARNOLD FRIBERG, *oil on canvas* (30 x 28), 1949. The Hudson's Bay blanket worn by the Mountie's companion and the accurate delineation of the canoe and the tepees point to Friberg's growing interest in depicting actual historical artifacts. Friberg sketched many such items during the 1960s in Browning, Montana.

HAROLD MICHAELSON,
oil on canvas (34 x 38), 1949.
A calendar subject, this work shows the
Mountie protecting the trapper on his
perilous trek to a trading post.

HAROLD MICHAELSON,
opaque watercolor (19½ x 29½), 1956.
A rare text-based ad from the 1950s,
this one comments on why the
Mountie in his canoe is pertinent
to the paper business: "Frequently, [a]
Prospect's conception of the
Manufacturer's product may be,
at long range, wholly dependent
upon the Printed Word." As the
canoe carries a season's furs,
so paper carries the sales message.

ARNOLD FRIBERG, *oil on canvas* (31 x 30), 1953. The trapper acquires a family in the 1950s, like TV's Ozzie Nelson or Jim Anderson.

ARNOLD FRIBERG,
oil on canvas (31 x 30), 1955.
Furs again: the Mountie receives a
magnificent buffalo robe from his
grateful charges. Within a generation, the
buffalo herd of North America would be gone.

HAROLD MICHAELSON,
oil on canvas (31 x 30), 1953.
During the early 1950s, the media and the
dimensions of the works used in the Northwest
campaign began to be standardized to fit the
format of a full-color vertical picture printed
on sample sheets of quality papers with almost
no text. Such sheets were inserted into trade
magazines. The pages were also distributed
independently for various promotional efforts.

WALTER OSCHMAN,
oil on canvas (31 x 30), 1954.
The Mountie serves as a referee,
making sure that the sellers receive
fair value from the buyers.

ARNOLD FRIBERG,
oil on canvas (30 x 28), 1950.
The trapper's trek to market
was fraught with danger.

ARNOLD FRIBERG,
oil on canvas (28 x 30), 1950.
The Mountie watches canoes pushing
for the nearest trading post.

ARNOLD
FRIBERG,
oil on canvas
(36 x 46), 1953.
This calendar plate for
1953 depicts another
trapper's cabin lost in
the snow and the
Mountie, painted at
heroic scale, setting out
to escort a hard-won
load of furs to market.

DᴇLOOY (?), *oil on canvas* (32 x 25), 1960. Out on the trail, the Mountie waves his arm to greet—the viewer, or a lonesome trapper?

THE MOUNTIE
DOMESTICATED

ARNOLD FRIBERG, *oil on canvas* (31 x 30), 1951. The natural habitat of the fictional
Mountie is the out-of-doors: pine forests, rippling streams, ducks soaring overhead.

ARNOLD FRIBERG, *oil on canvas* (31 x 30), 1955. With progress come the perils of avarice.

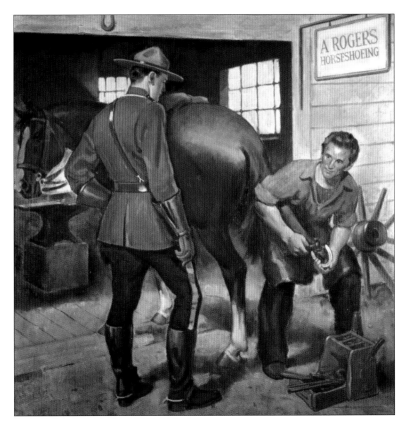

HAROLD MICHAELSON, *oil on canvas* (31 x 30), 1953. Yet progress also brings fellowship: towns, families, services, and a gentler way of life. Mr. Rogers chats amiably as he shoes the Mountie's horse.

ARNOLD FRIBERG, *oil on canvas* (31 x 30), 1953. The Mountie observes a painter at work; in the 1950s, the do-it-yourself movement and paint-by-number sets let every home owner become his or her own decorator.

WALTER OSCHMAN,
oil on canvas (29 x 28), 1950.
The symbolic peace pipe stands
for the new social order in the
postwar world.

WALTER OSCHMAN,
oil on canvas (31 x 30), 1953.
The Mountie is a prominent figure,
but the baby steals the scene.

WALTER OSCHMAN,
oil on panel (29 x 28), 1953.
Little Beaver and his dog have
had a successful hunt.

WALTER OSCHMAN,
oil on panel (31 x 30), 1954.
A woman's work is never done,
even on the trail. Oschman's
women, blond and busty, would
have been right at home in ads
for consumer products: beer,
lingerie, or washing machines.

DeLOOY (?), *oil on canvas* (32 x 25), 1958. The Mountie is always welcome in the Hollywood Indian village, where the totem poles of the Northwest Coast are out of place beside the tepees of the Plains.

ARNOLD FRIBERG, *oil on canvas* (32 x 24¾), 1957. He marries his flock and acts as preacher man too, reading Bible stories to a rapt audience.

WALTER OSCHMAN,
oil on canvas (31 x 30), 1954.
Grinding the corn and boiling the
meal: the theme evokes other ads—
for shiny, new color-coordinated
kitchen ranges and small appliances.

WALTER OSCHMAN,
oil on canvas (31 x 30), 1955.
The old prospector with his beautiful
collie ("Lassie"?) is also a member of
the Mountie's extended community.

HAROLD MICHAELSON,
oil on canvas (29 x 28), 1950.

ARNOLD FRIBERG,
oil on canvas (31 x 30), 1954.
Reissued on a 1976 calendar, the subject matter of this picture speaks to Friberg's ongoing fascination with Indian arts and crafts, especially the construction of canoes. He becomes the Mountie who observes the ancient technology with great interest.

ARNOLD FRIBERG, *oil on canvas* (31 x 30), 1952. Dressed for an Arctic spring—except for his coat, of course—the Mountie fishes with an Inuit child just outside an igloo village.

THE MOUNTIE ALWAYS GETS HIS MAN

HAROLD MICHAELSON, *oil on canvas* (25¼ x 26¼), 1948.

DeLOOY (?), *oil on canvas* (32 x 25), 1960.

ARNOLD FRIBERG, *oil on canvas* (32 x 25), 1962. This picture was reused on a Potlatch calendar in 1971.

ARNOLD FRIBERG,
pen-and-ink wash with opaque white
(19 x 17¼), 1955.

ARNOLD FRIBERG,
oil on canvas
(30 x 28), 1949.

ARNOLD FRIBERG, *oil on canvas* (31 x 30), 1956.

ARNOLD
FRIBERG,
oil on canvas
(40¼ x 51), 1951.

ARNOLD FRIBERG,
oil on canvas (38 x 48), 1954.

ARNOLD FRIBERG, *oil on canvas* (32 x 25), 1961.

ARNOLD FRIBERG, *oil on canvas* (36 x 46), 1956.

THE SAME MOUNTIE

A Search for New Imagery

ROBERT ADDISON, *oil on canvas* (31 x 30), 1956.

ARNOLD FRIBERG, *oil on canvas* (32 x 25), 1967.

ARNOLD FRIBERG, *oil on canvas* (32 x 25), 1967.

ARNOLD FRIBERG, *oil on canvas* (32 x 25), 1970.

ARNOLD FRIBERG, *oil on canvas* (32 x 25), undated.

ARNOLD FRIBERG, *oil on canvas* (32 x 25), undated.

ROBERT ADDISON, *oil on canvas* (32 x 25), 1957. This is a Hollywood Mountie who seems to have strayed far to the South.

ARNOLD FRIBERG, *oil on canvas* (32 x 25), 1965. The autumnal atmosphere of this harvest scene at sunset is as important as the Mountie.

ARNOLD FRIBERG, *oil on canvas* (32 x 25), 1970. Painted in the last official year of the Mountie campaign, this scene takes advantage of theatrical lighting and a colorful secondary character to add interest to the theme.

ARNOLD FRIBERG, SAFE PASSAGE, *oil on canvas* (32 x 25), 1967. In Friberg's later pictures from the series, the supporting cast becomes as interesting as the hero.

ROBERT ADDISON, *oil on canvas* (32 x 25), 1957. The extreme angle at which the train rushes headlong out of the picture is a Hollywood trick often used with locomotives. Cinematographer Gregg Toland once dug a trench under the track to photograph the oncoming train arriving and then thundering overhead.

ROBERT ADDISON, *oil on canvas* (32 x 25), 1958. The prominence of the beaver in the foreground anticipates the rise of bird and animal art in the hierarchy of popular genres, beginning in the 1950s and 1960s.

IRVIN "SHORTY" SHOPE, VISITORS IN CAMP, *oil on canvas* (32 x 25), 1960. Although a similar subject had been used earlier in the series, this example emphasizes excitement and a sense of made-for-TV adventure.

ROBERT ADDISON, *oil on canvas* (32 x 25), 1960. With the Western drama
dominating television, the cowboy becomes the Mountie's natural companion.

ARNOLD FRIBERG, *oil on canvas* (32 x 26), 1960.

IRVIN "SHORTY" SHOPE, WARNING OF DANGER, *oil on canvas* (32 x 25), 1960.
This is the kind of scene that helped shape the comic-book image of the Native American.

ARNOLD FRIBERG, MOUNTIE AT PIONEER'S GRAVE, *oil on panel* (32 x 25), 1960. Friberg here aims for the kind of sentiment that often marks the climax of the Western, where the solitary hero pauses at the grave of a lost love.

IRVIN "SHORTY" SHOPE, SUSPICIOUS CHARACTER, *oil on canvas* (32 x 25), 1960. In contrast to the simplicity of the early Mountie pictures, this one includes a little of everything: scenery, animals, Indian woodcraft, the Mountie, and a hint of drama.

ROBERT ADDISON, MOUNTIE AND FOREST FIRE, *oil on canvas* (32 x 25), 1960. Like Friberg, Addison and Shope frame their works as exciting narratives.

IRVIN "SHORTY" SHOPE, Red River Cart, *oil on canvas* (32 x 25), 1960.

IRVIN "SHORTY" SHOPE, MISSION ACCOMPLISHED, *oil on canvas* (32 x 25), 1960.

ARNOLD FRIBERG

The Essential Mountie

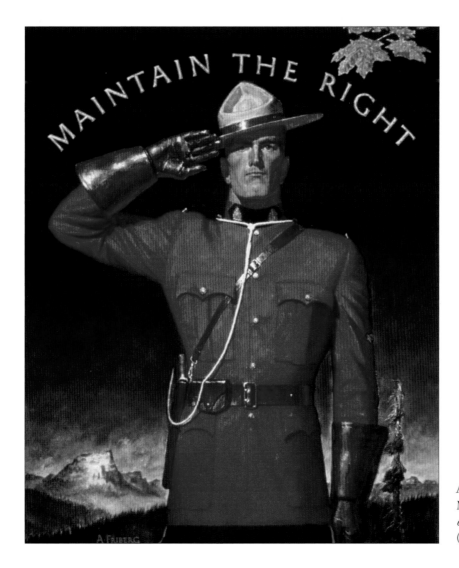

ARNOLD FRIBERG,
Maintain the Right,
oil on canvas
(32 x 25), 1963.

ARNOLD FRIBERG, Precarious Passage, *oil on canvas* (32 x 25), 1962.

ARNOLD FRIBERG, *oil on canvas* (25 x 32), 1970.

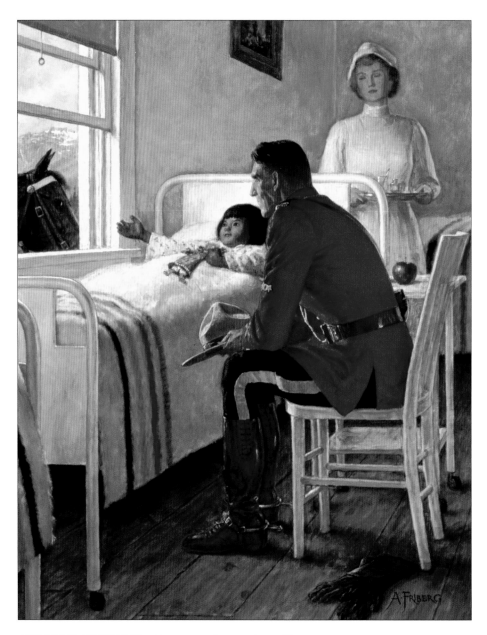

ARNOLD FRIBERG, *oil on canvas* (32 x 25), 1964.

ARNOLD FRIBERG, *oil on canvas* (32 x 25), 1965.

ARNOLD FRIBERG, *oil on canvas* (32 x 25), undated.

ARNOLD FRIBERG, *oil on canvas* (32 x 25), 1963.

ARNOLD FRIBERG, *opaque watercolor on board* (17 x 14), 1940.

III

THE ARTISTS

The Potlatch Collection
Tweed Museum of Art

ROBERT ADDISON

(1924–1988) was born in Boise, Idaho, and died in Chicago. After World War II, Addison produced a number of independent paintings in the regionalist or social-realist style, depicting Chicago street scenes. (14 Mountie paintings in Tweed Museum of Art collection, 1953–1962)

E. J. BOECHER

(1885–1951) was another Chicagoan who made a name for himself in religious art. In the 1920s, he worked for the Grauman studio. His Mountie pictures are cosigned with the name of the Bielefeld studio of Chicago. (2 Mountie subjects, 1937)

STUDLEY OLDHAM BURROUGHS

(1892–1949) was a nephew of novelist Edgar Rice Burroughs, creator of the Tarzan character. A Chicagoan, Burroughs did occasional advertising work for General Motors, Sunkist oranges, and other products in addition to illustrations for his uncle's books. The elder Burroughs had also approached Hal Foster and J. Allen St. John for Tarzan drawings, and it is perhaps through those artists that Studley came to work on the Mountie campaign. (3 Mountie subjects, 1935–1944)

BENTON CLARK

(1895–1964), a great admirer of Remington, studied illustration at the school of the Chicago Art Institute and later worked for the Stevens-Sundblom and Kling studios in Chicago. He was also employed for a time in the art department of MGM Pictures in Culver City, California. In the 1930s, his illustrations for *McCall's,* the *Saturday Evening Post,* and *Good Housekeeping* were well known. He is best remembered today, however, for his vivid paintings of the Wild West. (1 Mountie subject, 1943)

DeLOOY (?)

Known only by a signature that is difficult to decipher. (6 Mountie subjects, 1958–1960)

HAROLD R. (HAL) FOSTER

(1892–1981), a Canadian who rode a bicycle from Winnipeg to Chicago to enroll at the Art Institute and later at the Chicago Academy of Fine Arts, originally served as an assistant to J. Allen St. John. In the mid-1920s, Foster illustrated magazine covers, especially for *Popular Mechanics,* and developed a reputation for rendering men of action convincingly. As a result, he was chosen to illustrate the *Tarzan* comic strip and, in 1937, created the legendary

Sunday-only strip *Prince Valiant.* He was the first artist employed by the Frank Cash agency on the Northwest Paper account. (13 Mountie subjects, 1931–1945)

ARNOLD FRIBERG

(1913–) studied at the Chicago Academy of Fine Arts after enrolling in mail-order courses as a young teenager in Phoenix. Now known as a distinguished Western artist, Friberg in his early career was dominated by two influences. One was the Mountie project, for which he designed ads and calendars for more than forty years. The other was his collaboration with Cecil B. DeMille on *The Ten Commandments,* for which Friberg prepared costume designs, sketches used in framing the scenes, and oil paintings sent out on tour with the movie. In the 1960s, Friberg became a hero to the members of the Royal Canadian Mounted Police, thanks to his Northwest and Potlatch illustrations, and became an honorary member of the force in the early 1970s. In the course of a long career, Friberg also created a series of biblical paintings drawn from the *Book of Mormon,* a cycle of works on the history of intercollegiate football for General Motors, and a well-known painting of George Washington praying at Valley Forge for the American Bicentennial. Arnold Friberg lives and continues to paint in Salt Lake City, Utah. (200 Mountie subjects, 1937–1970)

FRANCES (FRANK) GODWIN

(1889–1959) was a Washingtonian who studied at New York's Art Students League and idolized James Montgomery Flagg and Charles Dana Gibson, East Coast cosmopolitans admired for their renderings of beautiful women. During the 1920s, Godwin's pen-and-ink drawings were featured in magazines, ads, and neo-medieval book illustrations heavily influenced by N. C. Wyeth and Maxfield Parrish. With the depression, Godwin became a syndicated strip cartoonist responsible for the *Connie* series and, eventually, for *Wonder Woman.* (2 Mountie subjects, 1942–1944)

BURNE HOGARTH

(1911–1996) enrolled at the Chicago Art Institute when he was only twelve and continued his studies at the Chicago Academy of Fine Arts. Primarily known as a brilliant and influential cartoonist, Hogarth took over the *Tarzan* strip from Hal Foster in 1937 and later published several books on anatomical illustration. (1 Mountie subject, 1945)

HAROLD MICHAELSON

(active 1940s–1990s) may be the New York- and Hollywood-based illustrator whose career centered on the film industry. Michaelson worked as a movie sketch artist; one of his earliest assignments was at Paramount, for Cecil B. DeMille's *The Ten Commandments*. His best-known job was as chief illustrator for Alfred Hitchcock's *The Birds*. (39 Mountie subjects, 1946–1953)

WALTER S. OSCHMAN

Oschman illustrated several books for children and an edition of Ralph Waldo Emerson's essays published in Chicago in 1949. (36 Mountie subjects, 1943–1960)

PAKINES (?)

An unreadable signature, possibly that of Frank O. King (born 1883), a Chicago Academy of Fine Arts alumnus whose most successful and longest-running comic strip was the syndicated *Gasoline Alley*. (1 Mountie subject, 1944)

PAUL PROEHL

(1887–1965) attended several Chicago art schools and began a lengthy career as an advertising artist in 1918. A partner at the Palenske Young studio, he specialized in action scenes of locomotives for the high-quality calendars issued by the Chicago and North Western railroad. Between 1948 and 1950, he worked in Hollywood for Columbia and RKO Pictures. (36 Mountie subjects, 1935–1946)

IRVIN "SHORTY" SHOPE

(1900–1978), a Western artist, lived and died in Montana; in 1935, he served as commercial artist for that state. After World War II, he largely gave up illustration in favor of paintings of the Old West. (11 Mountie subjects, 1959–1960)

J. ALLEN ST. JOHN

(1875–1960), a laureate of the Society of Illustrators Hall of Fame, studied in New York and France before moving to Chicago around 1912. The dean of the Chicago illustrators, he taught at the Art Institute and the Academy; Arnold Friberg was among his many pupils. St. John was associated with the *Tarzan* novels and with pulp fiction, Western tales, and storybooks published by Chicago firms. Commentators on his work believe that had he not worked primarily in the Midwest, he would today rank among the period's greatest and most versatile illustrators. (1 Mountie subject, 1944)

PAUL PROEHL, *watercolor* (26 x 18), 1942. Another stranger is stopped in his tracks by the keen-eyed Mountie. "Loose lips sink ships" was the poster motto reminding Americans not to talk about their war work in front of newcomers or people they did not know.

IRVIN "SHORTY" SHOPE, WHERE THE TRAIL DIVIDES, *oil on canvas* (32 x 25), 1960.

INDEX of ILLUSTRATIONS

By Artist

Book design by

Mary Susan Oleson

NASHVILLE, TENNESSEE

FONTS USED:
MISTRAL
AGARAMOND
ENGRAVERS, MT